CBT Toolbox

for Depressed, Anxious & Suicidal

Children and Adolescents

Over 220 Worksheets and
Therapist Tips to Manage Moods,
Build Positive Coping Skills &
Develop Resiliency

David M. Pratt, PhD, MSW

Copyright © 2019 by David M. Pratt

Published by
PESI Publishing & Media
PESI, Inc.
3839 White Ave
Eau Claire, WI 54703

Editing: Jenessa Jackson
Layout: Bookmasters & Amy Rubenzer
Cover: Amy Rubenzer
ISBN: 9781683732532

PESI
Publishing
& Media
pesipublishing.com

About the Author

David M. Pratt, PhD, MSW, is a New York State licensed psychologist with 40 years of clinical experience working with children, adolescents, and families. Dr. Pratt is in private practice at the Western New York Psychotherapy Services in Amherst, New York. Previously, he was the principal psychologist at the Western New York Children's Psychiatric Center, a clinical assistant professor of psychiatry at the University at Buffalo, and an adjunct professor/lecturer in the Department of Counseling, School, and Educational Psychology at Buffalo as well. He is presently on the training faculty with the School of Social Work at the University at Buffalo, and a member of the New York State Office of Mental Health Advisory Board on Evidence-Based Treatments for Youth. Dr. Pratt also presents seminars for PESI and has conducted numerous trainings and workshops in cognitive-behavioral therapy at local, state, national, and international forums.

Contents

Introduction

Welcome to the *CBT Toolbox for Depressed, Anxious and Suicidal Children and Adolescents*. This workbook is designed to give you – the mental health professional – a variety of practical therapy tools that you can use with child and adolescent clients who struggle with depression, anxiety, and suicidal urges.

Why I Wrote This Book

I developed this workbook over the past 20 years while working with severely emotionally disturbed children and teens in a psychiatric facility, as well as in my private practice. Doing therapy with young children and adolescents presents many challenges. These kids are often very "reluctant doers." They can be overwhelmed by their problems and highly mistrustful of even the most compassionate therapist. Reaching this population and engaging them in meaningful therapy is quite a challenge indeed.

During my time at Western New York Children's Psychiatric Center, I began developing a group therapy program for adolescents with significant depression, anxiety, and suicidality. I researched the existing evidence-based treatment programs for adolescent depression, identified the essential ingredients of successful treatment, and began to develop my own structured therapeutic activities (Clarke, Lewinsohn, & Hops, 1990; Curry et al., 2000). My co-therapist and I weren't sure what was going to happen when we introduced these activities in group therapy, but we thought it was worth a try. Believe me when I say that we were ready to duck! But to our surprise (and great relief), the kids responded really well. They actually came to group, participated in the activities, and began to self-disclose intimate details of their lives and struggles. And, our post-group anonymous satisfaction surveys showed they both enjoyed and benefited from the group!

What I learned is that when treatment is presented in a manner that children can relate to and are comfortable with, they are quite willing to engage in productive therapy. Kids have a schema for doing structured learning activities from their experiences in school, and we based our exercises on this model. Using a psychoeducational format, we taught these kids a variety of skills and helped them practice these skills together in a supportive group. We didn't let them sit in group and be befuddled by open-ended, unstructured therapy questions, like one might do in a "process group." Rather, we relied heavily on the use of structured paper/pencil worksheets and role-play exercises. We praised every approximation of appropriate therapy participation, and they responded magnificently.

Myself and various co-therapists ran this group many years. We continuously researched and revised our material, and gradually developed a treatment manual called the "Mood Management Program" (Pratt, 2008). The *CBT Toolbox for Depressed, Anxious and Suicidal Children and Adolescents* is the product of this 20-year process. I hope you will find this workbook as helpful with your clients as I did with mine. Use the workbook wisely (and always with a healthy dose of compassion and optimism), and chances are you will reach a lot of kids and be rewarded beyond your imagination.

What's Inside?

This workbook contains over 100 evidence-based, structured, youth-friendly therapeutic handouts and activities that children and adolescents can use to build positive coping skills and develop resiliency in the face of depression, anxiety, and self-harm urges. These activities are based on traditional cognitive-behavioral therapy (CBT) approaches that have also been integrated with more recent "third wave" mindfulness practices. The activities in this workbook can be used in individual or group formats and across a variety of treatment settings, including inpatient treatment, day treatment, residential settings, mental health clinics, private practice, pediatric practice, and school settings. Perhaps most appealing, these are activities that kids find engaging, understandable, and helpful.

The structure of the workbook is organized into the following 13 chapters:

- **Chapter 1: Therapist Guidelines** – No matter how well-developed this workbook is, the tools provided here will not be helpful in the absence of a strong therapeutic relationship and without the flexible application by an empathic and skilled therapist. This chapter provides you with guidelines for applying the tools in this workbook in a sensitive, individualized, and effective manner.

- **Chapter 2: Psychoeducation** – All too often, there is a stigma associated with seeking treatment for mental-health related issues, especially among kids. This chapter provides children and adolescents with psychoeducation regarding depression and anxiety with the hope that this information will reduce any associated stigma and empower them to engage in treatment. Written in readily understandable language, these psychoeducation materials help kids and their parents understand the complex principles behind CBT that lead to successful treatment.

- **Chapter 3: Goal Setting and Motivational Counseling** – Youth rarely initiate counseling on their own or have mature insight and motivation for treatment. Motivating kids to engage in and commit to treatment is almost always necessary. In addition, therapy rarely progresses in the absence of relevant, mutually-defined treatment goals. This chapter discusses goal setting and motivational counseling to help you engage the cautious youth in focused treatment.

- **Chapter 4: Mindfulness** – The tools in this chapter teach kids about the neuroscience of stress, including how the brain reacts to stress. A dozen youth-friendly mindfulness practices are included in this chapter, with detailed instructions for guiding children and adolescents in utilizing mindfulness skills to calm the emotional part of their brain and utilize the rational, problem-solving part of their brain.

- **Chapter 5: Mood Monitoring** – Self-awareness is a critical coping skill in life and is often lacking with troubled youth. In this chapter, a variety of tools are provided to help children and adolescents develop greater awareness of their feelings, including their ability to identify triggers and rate the intensity of their feelings. They are also provided with mood monitoring logs to help them become aware of patterns in their mood and the triggers that impact their mood.

- **Chapter 6: Behavioral Activation** – Research shows that behavioral activation is an effective intervention for depression, anxiety, and suicide prevention. Therefore, this chapter focuses on helping kids become more involved in healthy social and recreational activities they truly value. Young clients are encouraged to develop "behavioral experiments" to see how engaging in new behaviors impacts their mood.

- **Chapter 7: Cognitive Processing** – This chapter helps children and adolescents become aware of their negative, subconscious thoughts. Through education and structured activities, they are taught to identify trigger situations and their subsequent "stinking thinking." They are also taught how this stinking thinking impacts their feelings and behaviors.

- **Chapter 8: Cognitive Restructuring** – Cognitive restructuring is the "sine qua non" of CBT, meaning that it is an essential component of treatment. However, replacing maladaptive thoughts with healthier, more adaptive thoughts is a complex meta-cognitive task that can be quite difficult for kids to grasp and utilize. This chapter provides a number of youth-friendly methods to challenge and replace stinking thinking with more realistic, positive thinking.

- **Chapter 9: Social Skills Training** – Kids who are depressed, anxious, and suicidal are often lacking critical social skills. This chapter helps children and adolescents learn effective problem-solving, assertiveness, communication, and friendship skills to improve their social relationships and make them more resilient in the face of stress.

- **Chapter 10: Anxiety Treatment and Exposure Therapy** – Children and adolescents who struggle with anxiety often avoid anxiety-provoking emotions and situations in order to feel better in the short term, despite the long-term consequences of doing so. This chapter teaches kids the skills needed to face their fears in a gradual and competent manner through the use of exposure therapy, which is an essential ingredient in the treatment of anxiety.

- **Chapter 11: Special Topics in Treating Anxiety** – This chapter is an extension of Chapter 10, in that it describes how to use the basic elements of exposure therapy with select anxiety disorders, including: social anxiety, separation anxiety, generalized anxiety disorder, and somatic symptom disorder.

- **Chapter 12: Managing Self-harm and Suicidal Urges** – Kids who are depressed and anxious are at greater risk for despair, hopelessness, and suicide. This chapter provides you with the knowledge and skills needed to conduct a competent suicide risk assessment and develop an evidence-based safety plan. In addition, a variety of structured therapeutic activities are included to teach self-harm and suicide prevention skills.

- **Chapter 13: Parent Involvement** – It is not only kids with depression, anxiety, and suicidality who are suffering – their parents are suffering as well and need our active support. This chapter discusses how to involve parents in the psychoeducation, assessment, diagnosis, case conceptualization, treatment planning, and therapy process. In addition, several structured, evidence-based therapeutic activities are included to improve family functioning.

In addition, the handouts and worksheets in each chapter are preceded by a Therapist Tips section that provides you with practical guidelines and suggestions for implementing each structured activity. These tips can help you to more effectively engage your clients and increase their chances of therapeutic success.

Why You Need This Workbook

It can be difficult to engage children and adolescents in the treatment process. By using the evidence-based, structured therapeutic activities in this workbook, you can present treatment in a more relatable manner and help kids learn practical skills to manage depression, anxiety, and self-harm or suicide urges. It is my hope that this workbook will enhance your clinical skills and help you offer the high quality treatment children and adolescents both need and deserve.

Acknowledgements

I am truly grateful to the many people who have nurtured, stimulated and supported me throughout my life and by virtue of their support have contributed to this book. Regrettably, I am unable to acknowledge all of those who have helped me along the way. I hope those not mentioned will understand and appreciate the following people who stand out among the many who deserve recognition.

First and foremost, I'd like to thank my parents Eugene and Marie Pratt. I was so fortunate to have them as parents. They nurtured and supported me while providing a stable and enriched early life experience. They encouraged humanistic values, education and perhaps most importantly my autonomy and confidence. Thanks mom and dad!

I am grateful beyond words to my wife of nearly 40 years, Celia Spacone, Ph.D., who through her love and support has enriched me and helped me create an adult life that is beyond what I ever imagined possible. I doubt that the joy I have experienced in my life would have ever occurred without her loving presence. Foremost among the joys in my life are my two children, Justin and Andrea. They brought a level of happiness and "raison d'etre" that surely contributed to my capacity to write this book. Without question, this book would not have been written in the absence of the love and joy I have experienced through my wife and children. I can't thank you enough!

So many others have also inspired me and contributed to this accomplishment. Many thanks to my brother, E. Douglas Pratt, DSW, with whom I have had many stimulating clinical discussions. Kathleen Denny Leatherbarrow, NP, deserves special recognition for helping me recognize my enthusiasm and calling for child psychology in my college days. I can't thank my doctoral studies mentor, James C. Hansen, Ph.D., enough for the confidence he had in me and the support provided throughout my doctoral studies. We lost him much too early. Eternal peace and thanks, Dr. Hansen. Special thanks to Gary N. Cohen, MD, who hired me not once, not twice but thrice in my career and gave me the opportunity to grow and thrive as a young professional. I would be terribly remiss to not mention Lesa Fichte, LMSW, ACSW, who has been so instrumental in helping me develop my interest in clinical training. And, I am so appreciative of all the great clinicians and students who were co-therapists with me over many years and who helped me develop the clinical material that gave rise to this book, most notably, Catherine Heimback-Murdie, LCSW-R, and Susan LaGraves, LCSW-R.

I wish to thank the wonderful staff at PESI, Inc. most notably Emily Krumenauer, Linda Jackson, Jenessa Jackson, Ph.D., and Joy Hurlburt. Thank you all for your wonderful editorial assistance and enthusiasm for this book.

Finally, I'd like to thank all of the brave clients I've worked with throughout my career for helping me remain humble and teaching me so much. I hope your journey was enhanced by our connection. I know mine was.

David M. Pratt, Ph.D., MSW

CHAPTER ONE

Therapist Guidelines:
Keys to Successful CBT

At its core, the emphasis of CBT involves altering cognitions and behaviors (Beck, Rush, Shaw, & Emery, 1979). The theory behind the treatment is quite simple: Change a client's thoughts and/or behaviors, and there will be a resultant change in his or her mood. This process sounds straightforward in theory, and often our temptation as therapists is to naively direct clients to think and behave in a certain manner, and expect them to dutifully follow our well-intended advice and then feel better. If it were only so simple. In reality, this type of approach is rarely effective, and it is critical that you do not fall into this trap.

Treatment workbooks can give therapists the false illusion that all they need to do is present the content outlined in the workbook and the client will get better. This is far from being the case. An effective therapist must use a treatment workbook and its content in a manner that facilitates the therapeutic relationship toward a successful treatment outcome. This is more likely to occur if the therapist remains mindful of the following nine principles:

1. **The therapeutic relationship is key:** Psychotherapy research has shown that the quality of the therapeutic relationship is just as important as the specific treatment method in predicting treatment outcome (Wampold & Imel, 2015). That is, relationship factors – such as empathy, genuineness, unconditional positive regard, emotional support, respect, and working with a person's strengths – are just as important as the specific therapeutic method that is employed. This is not to say that the therapeutic method is not important. Indeed, CBT has been shown to be a very effective treatment for many mental health conditions among children and adolescents, most notably depression and anxiety (Weisz & Kazdin, 2017). However, it is critical that clinicians understand that this workbook, or any treatment workbook, no matter how well-developed, will not be helpful in the absence of a positive therapeutic relationship.

2. **Kids relate well to structured therapeutic activities:** Doing psychotherapy with children and adolescents is a challenging process. Very few kids initiate therapy, and it's the rare child or teen who has a natural capacity for trust, self-awareness, and self-disclosure. It has been my experience that most kids do not respond well to an unstructured discussion of their struggles with a therapist. Most kids are likely to be inhibited in this type of "grown-up" discussion format.

    In contrast, I have found that the vast majority of youth are much more comfortable and willing to self-disclose in a structured format that parallels the didactic format used in schools. Kids have a schema for structured handouts and worksheets from their experiences in school, which makes them more comfortable using these types of structured exercises in the therapy process as well. In my own experience, I have found kids to be much more willing to disclose intimate details regarding their personal life via a structured worksheet than through unstructured self-exploration. By using the structured materials in this workbook, you can provide kids with a more familiar and safer method for self-exploration, discovery, self-disclosure, and change.

3. **Be flexible and individualize treatment:** One potential pitfall of any treatment workbook is trying to implement its curriculum using a rigid "one-size-fits-all" approach. We all realize that our clients are individuals with unique problems. It is only fitting that we provide treatment in an individualized manner that is appropriate to their unique problems and needs. When using this workbook, it is important not to make the mistake of applying the treatment curriculum in a linear, sequential manner. While there is a certain logic to the presentation of the material in this workbook, there is no sacrosanct rule regarding how or when the material should be presented.

    For example, in many cases, it is desirable to begin treatment with psychoeducation, given that "knowledge is power." Indeed, it is for this reason that a chapter on psychoeducation is prioritized earlier in the workbook. However, some clients may present to treatment in the midst of a crisis and may need help learning certain select skills to manage the emergent crisis. Other clients may need more work on a subset of skills focused on their unique problem while needing less attention to other skills in the workbook. The point is that each client will have his or her unique set of priorities, and the adroit therapist will be aware of this and present material that is designed to meet these specific needs.

4. **Collaboration and transparency build the therapeutic alliance:** Transparency and collaboration are essential elements of CBT. Transparency means that, as a therapist, you are willing to share various aspects of your clinical thinking and intervene with clients in an open and respectful manner. This may include sharing your case conceptualization, diagnosis, and various treatment recommendations with the child or adolescent. Collaboration refers to your commitment to work together with clients to help them resolve their concerns. CBT in particular is known for "collaborative empiricism," in which therapists work together with the client to gather data to examine the accuracy of specific clinical hypotheses and interventions.

    In order to foster a positive therapeutic relationship, transparency and collaboration must go hand-in-hand. That is, transparency in the absence of true collaboration is likely to be detrimental to the therapeutic process – and, conversely, true collaboration is not possible without transparency. For example, when being transparent about a clinical hypothesis or treatment recommendation, it is critical to ask for the client's feedback to see if he or she agrees and sees it the same way. It's vitally important in such situations to remain humble and ask the client, "Do you think I got this right?" Asking this question and being truly open to the client's feedback is being both transparent and collaborative. Likewise, a collaborative therapist will invite clients to do a "behavioral experiment" to test out a clinical intervention discussed in the treatment session. A truly collaborative therapist will remain open to the client's willingness to do the "experiment," as well as the client's response to the "experiment."

5. **Maintain a Socratic posture:** Cognitive restructuring is a primary intervention in CBT. Although it may be readily apparent to the therapist how a child's cognitive distortions ("stinking thinking")

are negatively impacting them and maintaining their depression or anxiety, the client has "blind spots" and likely does not recognize this stinking thinking as readily as the therapist. What's key here is maintaining a Socratic position vis-à-vis the client. That is, therapists should never tell clients that their thinking is not logical, nor should they ever tell clients the "right" way to think. Doing so is quite condescending and likely to be rejected by most clients, including kids. Instead, ask strategic "Socratic" questions to help clients think for themselves and assess whether or not their thinking or interpretations are accurate and helpful. The structured activities in this workbook are designed to help clients with this self-analysis and discovery. As the therapist, your job is to facilitate "guided discovery" by using these structured activities while maintaining a respectful Socratic posture.

6. **Remain genuinely curious:** One of our primary goals as therapists is to help our clients become self-aware and reveal themselves to us. The structured activities in this workbook are designed to do just that. The key is to allow this to happen by remaining genuinely curious – *not* by forming premature conclusions regarding your clinical hypotheses about the client. These clinical hypotheses are just that: hypotheses. They remain hypotheses until they are confirmed by the client. For example, we may have a clinical hypothesis that a child is socially anxious and avoidant because he believes he is awkward and fears peer rejection if he exposes himself socially. This is a perfectly legitimate hypothesis, and it may be accurate. However, we must be open to the possibility that it isn't correct until it is confirmed by the child's self-disclosure. The structured activities in this workbook are intended to help that child become self-aware of this underlying fear and disclose this to us. However, this disclosure is more likely to happen when we remain genuinely curious and allow clients to tell their unique story and gradually reveal themselves to us.

7. **Do behavioral experiments:** Although it is necessary for clients to learn the skills taught in treatment in order for change to occur, this is only one component of the change process. In order for meaningful change to fully occur, these skills must also be translated outside of session. Conducting a behavioral experiment is a useful way to help clients accomplish this task, as it involves having them apply and generalize these skills to the real world (Satterfield, 2015). For example, a child who struggles socially could try smiling more and making eye contact with peers to see how these novel behaviors affect his or her social relationships. Or, a child with a specific cognitive distortion could go out and collect information to test the accuracy of this particular way of thinking. Doing a behavioral experiment exemplifies collaboration. Rather than advising clients on how to act or think, you invite them to do an experiment and check it out for themselves.

8. **Trust the process:** Psychotherapy is a process. Good outcomes occur when there is a good therapy process. Very often, therapists are too focused on the goal of "fixing" the problem, but this is often a clinical mistake. Focusing on facilitating a therapeutic process is much more likely to result in a successful therapy outcome. Although the materials in this workbook are designed to teach your young clients the skills needed to manage depression, anxiety, and suicidal urges, the focus should not be on "fixing" them. Rather, the goal is to help your clients develop the skills and competencies needed to better manage life. Resolution of specific problems will come naturally – and often in ways that you unimagined as your clients learn how to use the skills presented in treatment. Therefore, it is much more productive to focus on the process of building skills than to focus on an urgent need to "fix" a problem "du jour."

9. **Working with comorbidity:** Comorbidity is the norm when working with children and adolescents. Not only are anxiety and depression highly comorbid, but both of these conditions

are likely to coincide with one or more additional diagnoses, such as oppositional defiant disorder, attention-deficit/hyperactivity disorder, or a substance use disorder. Unfortunately, treatment of these comorbid conditions is beyond the scope of this workbook, as this workbook was specifically developed to facilitate the treatment process with depressed, anxious, and suicidal youth. It was not designed for, and may not be helpful for, youth presenting with other mental health conditions. However, the good news is that there are other well-developed, evidence-based treatments for most of these conditions (Weisz & Kazdin, 2017). The responsible clinician will research and develop competence in treating these common comorbidities and learn to integrate these treatments with their depressed and anxious clients.

When working with children and adolescents, therapy is a challenging process, even for the experienced therapist. Regardless of the evidence base of any treatment workbook, using the workbook's content in an artful manner is much more important. As you read on through the remainder of this workbook, remain mindful of the therapist guidelines outlined in this chapter.

By following these guidelines, you can build and maintain a therapeutic relationship with child and adolescent clients, and increase the chances of therapeutic success.

CHAPTER TWO

Psychoeducation:
Knowledge is Power

Psychoeducation is a mainstay of CBT. Knowledge is power, right? The more we know about a health issue, the better we can manage it. Helping kids understand depression and anxiety will help them be more knowledgeable and more committed to working in treatment and fighting it. Spending time early in treatment discussing the prevalence, causes, and treatments of depression and anxiety will help dispel any misconceptions that your young clients may have, and it will allow them to gain factual knowledge that will empower them in their treatment.

In addition to providing information about the disorders themselves, psychoeducation should include information regarding CBT and how it works. Research shows (Fennell & Teasdale, 1987) the client's belief that the treatment is plausible and likely to help them accounts for over half of the outcome in psychotherapy. Thus clients who understand their treatment and believe it will be helpful are much more likely to benefit from the treatment. Children and adolescents alike will benefit from knowing that CBT is an evidence-based treatment with vast research support. When kids understand how treatment works, they can make a truly informed decision to engage in the process. It also allows them to gain confidence in you and see you as a knowledgeable and competent clinician who can help them, which goes a long way in fostering a genuine therapeutic alliance.

This chapter provides you with psychoeducation materials to help your child and adolescent clients understand depression and anxiety, including how CBT can help with these conditions. The material is written in youth-friendly language that you can read together and discuss with your clients. These educational materials are best shared with parents as well, seeing as parents are your clients just as much as the child is.

Parents are instrumental in supporting the on-going treatment that their child needs, so they will benefit from understanding their child's condition and how CBT can help. Involving the parents in the psychoeducation process also facilitates the development of a therapeutic alliance and helps parents support the treatment you are doing with their child.

Why Psychoeducation?

- Explain how understanding a general health problem (like diabetes) can help people cope with it better and how this is true for mental health conditions (anxiety and depression) as well.

- Help children and adolescents (and their parents) understand that "knowledge is power."

- Be frank and open with this dialogue. Doing so will help reduce stigma and model good communication.

- Be careful not to call this "psycho" education when discussing this with your clients. Some children may think you are calling them a "psycho" (I learned this the hard way!). Best to refer to this simply as "education" when discussing with your clients and their parents.

Handout

Why Education?

. . . .

The more you know about a problem, the better chance you have to fix it, right?

This is especially true with some medical problems. Let's say a kid just found out he has diabetes. Diabetes is a bummer, but it can be managed well if you learn what diabetes is and what to do that helps.

Kids with diabetes have to take medicine (insulin) several times a day, often by a "shot" or a small "pump" that's hooked up to their body. They also have to watch what they eat because too much, or too little, sugar in their body can make them really sick.

There is a lot to know if you have diabetes – but the more you know, the better you will be able to manage it and have good life.

The same is true about anxiety and depression. The more you know about what anxiety and depression are, what causes them, and how to manage them, the better you will be able to manage them and have a good life!

So, that's what we are going to do in this lesson. We're going to learn what anxiety and depression are and how to manage them. Let's get started!

Depression and Anxiety Education

- Read the "Depression Education" and "Anxiety Education" passages together with your clients. Take turns reading each paragraph out loud.

- After each paragraph, pause and discuss the passage. Prompt your clients for understanding by asking questions and offering examples to clarify material.

- Be mindful that some kids may have difficulty reading and may not want to read out loud. For clients who have underdeveloped reading skills, it is best if you read the passage to them instead.

- With young children, it may be preferable to read the materials with the child's parent present. Young children may feel more secure when their parent is around, and the parent will benefit from this information as well.

- In contrast, adolescent clients may prefer to read the information without their parent present. They may also feel more comfortable discussing the material and asking questions with you if their parent is not in the room. Encourage adolescents to discuss the information with their parent in a joint meeting (after initially discussing it with you), or at home in between sessions.

- Not every child will need psychoeducation on both depression and anxiety. Make sure to base your review of these materials on the child's specific needs.

- Ask your clients to obtain a pocket folder for your CBT work together and have them bring it to each session. You can then give clients a copy of the handouts and worksheets to keep in the folder for future reference.

Handout

Depression Education

. . . .

What Are the Signs of Depression?

When people get depressed, they feel sad nearly every day. Oftentimes, instead of feeling sad, they can also feel angry or grouchy. They don't have much energy, and they lose interest in doing fun stuff. They often feel bad about themselves and have low self-esteem. Oftentimes, they don't sleep well. They might gain or lose weight. When teens are depressed, they feel like they've been bad or done something wrong. They might feel like things are hopeless and will never get better. Sometimes, they self-harm or think about ending their life.

Do Many Teens Get Depressed?

Research shows that about 12.5% of teenagers (or roughly 3 million adolescents) experienced depression in 2015. That means if a school has 1,000 kids, there will be about 125 kids with depression in that school! That's a lot of kids! Did you think it would be that many? Given those kinds of numbers, you are not the only depressed kid in your school.

What Causes Depression?

There are many reasons why kids get depressed. One of the causes is biological. For example, there is research that shows that depression can be due to an imbalance of certain chemicals in the brain, which are called "neurotransmitters" (especially serotonin, norepinephrine, and dopamine). Scientists have also found that depression runs in families, so there is a genetic link. So, biological factors contribute to depression, but there are other things that cause depression too.

Stress Can Cause Depression

One of the biggest causes of depression is stress. Stress happens when there are problems you just can't solve. You feel tense and upset a lot because the problems just don't get better. Stress can come from family problems, problems getting along with other kids, living in a poor neighborhood with crime, losing someone (like the death of a loved one, a friend moving away, or the end of a romantic relationship), school or legal problems, or being abused.

Negative Self-Talk Makes Depression Worse

Kids who are depressed tend to see things in very negative ways. They start thinking a lot of negative stuff over and over in their head. They think they're no good, that their life stinks, and that things will never get better. This is what we call "stinking thinking," and it only makes people feel even more depressed. Although it *is* very hard to keep a positive attitude when you are depressed, research shows that learning to remain positive (even when things are not going well) is helpful in overcoming depression.

Depression Treatments: Medication

What do we do to help kids who are depressed? Well, sometimes medicine helps balance out those brain chemicals we talked about earlier. (Remember, they are called neurotransmitters!) Some teens take medication, called antidepressants, to help their depression. Research shows that kids with moderate to severe depression may need medication, as well as counseling.

Talk Therapy Helps Too

Kids can reduce depression when they learn how to handle stress better. One way to do this is through a type of counseling called "cognitive-behavioral therapy" or "CBT" for short. In CBT, you will learn how to work toward positive goals. You will learn how to relax and be calm. You will learn to be aware your feelings, and you'll learn that you feel better when you are doing positive, healthy activities. You'll also learn how to replace your stinking thinking with some positive self-talk. You'll learn the skills needed to solve problems and improve your social skills, which can even help you get along better with your parents and family. Finally, you'll learn how to manage any urges that you might have to harm yourself, if that has been a problem for you. Research shows that CBT helps a lot of kids overcome depression. So, let's get started!

Handout

Anxiety Education

. . . .

Anxiety is Adaptive

Anxiety is a fancy word for feeling afraid, and it is a normal part of life. We all feel anxious or scared at times, and it is helpful to our survival. Did you know that a long time ago when there were cave men and women, our bodies developed the fight-or-flight response? This response was intended to help us survive dangerous situations. For example, when a cave man was attacked by a lion, he had to either fight the lion or run away. That's no easy task, right?

How Does the Fight-or-Flight Response Work?

When that cave man went into fight-or-flight mode, his body automatically reacted by making a chemical called "adrenalin." This made his heart beat faster so lots of blood could pump to his muscles and make them stronger. He also started breathing really fast so he could get lots of oxygen, and his eyes and ears were on high alert so he could see and hear any little sign of danger. We all have this same automatic fight-or-flight system in our body that turns on when we sense danger. This automatic system protects us, but sometimes it misfires ... and that's what causes an anxiety problem!

What Causes Anxiety to Misfire?

Sometimes, this automatic system misfires because we are born with a super sensitive one. Or, sometimes it misfires because something really scared us in the past and now we are extra sensitive to anything that reminds us of that experience. For example, if someone was in a car accident, they might get really scared whenever they have to get into a car. Once this automatic anxiety system starts, it's really hard to turn it off.

Anxiety Leads to Avoidance

Another reason that normal anxiety can become a problem has to do with the way that we all tend to act when we are afraid of something. Think about it ... What do we all tend to do when we are afraid of something? That's right, we avoid it! However, avoidance is a real problem. This is how it works:

> At first, it feels really good when you can avoid something that makes you nervous, right? For example, you're supposed to have a test at school, but there is a big blizzard and you get a snow day. As a result, you feel great because there is no test and you get to sleep in and chill all day.

Negative Reinforcement Plays a Role

We feel really good when we get to avoid something that we are nervous about or scared of. We have a fancy name for this good feeling, which is called "negative reinforcement." This negative reinforcement feels so good that it makes us want to avoid our fears, even when they are really not such a big deal. We just keep on avoiding and avoiding, and the anxiety problem never gets solved. It's tough to get over an anxiety problem because it feels so good to avoid it! Get it?

Negative Self-Talk Makes Anxiety Worse

Another reason why it's so hard to get over an anxiety problem is that our imagination gets the best of us when we are scared of something. You know, that stuff we say to ourselves in our head when we are nervous. Like you see in a cartoon, it's the stuff that's in the bubble over the person's head. It's what the person is really thinking, but usually not saying. Things like, "I'm going sound so stupid if the teacher makes me read my paper to the class … They're all going to laugh at me."

And you know what, we have a fancy name for this too! We call it "negative self-talk" (or "stinking thinking"). The problem is, negative self-talk is really a bit of an exaggeration. But we believe it anyway, and it makes us even more afraid. We just talk ourselves into feeling more and more afraid. Then, we avoid the scary stuff even more, and round-n-round we go.

But, there is good news. We know how to help kids with anxiety problems! And this is how we do it.

Anxiety Treatment: Exposure Therapy

You have to learn to face the things that scare you rather than avoid them. But don't worry, we do this really gradually. You face the things that scare you little by little. You start with things that you're just a little afraid of and gradually move up to the scarier stuff. We also go at your pace, so you're in control. If you can learn to face the stuff that scares you little by little, then you'll get used to it and see that it really isn't as scary as you thought it was, and the fear will gradually go away!

Other Components of Anxiety Treatment

Yep, psychologists have a fancy name for this too, it's called *gradual exposure*! So, we'll figure out a gradual way to face the things that you're afraid of one step at a time. But first, you'll learn some skills to manage your anxiety. You'll learn how to relax by breathing really slow and deep so that the automatic fight-or-flight response doesn't kick in. You'll learn how to think positive thoughts in your head so your negative self-talk doesn't freak you out. Then, you'll learn how to solve problems effectively and develop positive social skills. Once you have these tools, you'll be able to fight anxiety and win! As you get over your fears, you'll feel great about yourself, and your parents will be really proud of you too!

Therapist Tips

What is CBT?

- CBT is a common-sense treatment that can be readily explained to even a young child.

- Explain that for every situation in life, we all experience thoughts and feelings, which influence our behaviors.

- Give a simple, age-appropriate example of the relationship between thoughts, feelings and behaviors, such as the example included on the following handout.

- Explain that people can feel better (e.g., less depressed or anxious) by either changing their thoughts or behaviors. Provide a simple, age-appropriate example here as well.

- Let your clients know that you will help them learn how to change their thoughts and/or behaviors in CBT.

- Help parents understand CBT by sharing this information with them in session as well.

- If the parent does not attend the session, ask your clients to discuss the CBT educational materials at home with their parents. This will bring the absent parent into the process and help the child review the information again.

What is CBT?

. . . .

For every situation in life, we all experience thoughts and feelings, which influence our behaviors. For example, the day before a math test, a kid might be feeling nervous, and he might be thinking, "I stink at math, so what's the use in studying?" As a result, he might decide to blow off studying and play video games instead. In turn, he might end up doing poorly on the test. See, for every situation, we have thoughts and feelings, which cause us to behave a certain way.

If you are in a tough situation and feeling upset, you can cope with the situation and feel better by changing your thinking and/or your behavior. For example, if you have a math test tomorrow and are feeling nervous, instead of thinking that you're going to fail, you could think, "I've passed math tests before. I can pass this one too if I study hard." (This is positive thinking.) Then, instead of playing video games, you could study hard. (This is a positive behavior.) You'll probably feel more confident and do better on the test if you have positive thinking and engage in positive behaviors.

That is how CBT works: It teaches you new ways of thinking and behaving in order to help you feel better. It helps you learn how to have positive thinking and engage in positive behaviors to handle problems. This is what we are going to work on, so let's get started!

Education Review

- Encourage your clients to write down what they have learned about depression, anxiety, and CBT.

- Explain how repetition will enhance their learning.

- Review the psychoeducation materials at the beginning of the subsequent session.

- Encourage your clients to read the psychoeducation materials with their parent (if the client did not already do so in session or if the parent was unable to attend the session).

- Given that not every child will have been provided with psychoeducation on both depression and anxiety, make sure to tailor the following worksheet based on each child's specific needs.

Education Review

· ·

It's important to know what depression and anxiety are. The more you know about these conditions, the better you will be able to fight them. Write down what you have learned about depression and anxiety. Then, write about how CBT can help. Share and discuss this information with your parents. Remember, the more you know about depression and anxiety and how CBT works, the stronger you will be!

1. What are the signs of depression and anxiety? _____

   _____

   _____

2. How common is depression? _____

   _____

   _____

3. What are the causes of depression? _____

   _____

   _____

4. How do we help kids who have depression? _____

   _____

   _____

5. How does CBT help fight depression? _____

   _____

   _____

6. With anxiety, what is the fight-or-flight response? _____

_____

_____

7. What do people usually do when they are afraid of something? _____

_____

_____

8. How does avoiding the thing we are scared of make anxiety worse? _____

_____

_____

9. What is "negative self-talk" and how does it contribute to anxiety? _____

_____

_____

10. How do we help kids who have an anxiety problem? _____

_____

_____

11. Who is in charge of how fast you go when you face your fears? _____

_____

_____

12. What does "CBT" stand for? _____

_____

_____

13. What are the **three things** we all experience for every situation in life?

_____

_____

_____

14. In CBT, what **two things** do you need to change in order to feel better?

_____

_____

CHAPTER THREE

Goal Setting and Motivational Counseling:

Are You and Your Client Working Together?

Children and adolescents rarely initiate therapy on their own, and they often need our assistance with motivation and identifying relevant, specific treatment goals. The tools in this chapter will help you motivate your young clients by identifying mutually-defined treatment goals. Mutually-agreed upon treatment goals are an essential component of productive therapy because treatment won't progress if you and your clients are working on different goals. To avoid running into roadblocks, it is important to ensure that treatment goals are explicit and that you and your clients are on the same page.

When working with younger clients, I often use the following analogy in order to emphasize the importance of developing mutually-defined goals: I tell my young clients that if we are in a row boat and want to reach a specific spot on the other shore, the best thing to do is to row together in a coordinated fashion. Doing so will help us stay in a straight line and reach the other shore in the quickest time. However, if we row in opposite directions, we'll just go in circles and never reach the desired destination. In this same manner, developing mutually-defined treatment goals will help them reach their goals faster and more effectively.

Given that motivation and goal setting are intimately linked, helping your clients identify treatment goals will also increase their motivation for treatment. However, it is important to ensure that these goals are well-defined, as it can be difficult for clients to attain goals that are too broad or open-ended in nature. In order to help your clients attain their goals, you can help them turn their broader goals into "SMART" goals that are specific, measurable, attainable, realistic, and timely. Doing so helps you and your client stay on course, and it provides a template to evaluate their progress along the way.

In addition, you can enhance motivation to engage in treatment by asking them to look at the consequences of the current problem, analyzing the pros and cons of counseling, and identifying the potential benefits of treatment.

Why Goals Are Important

- Describe why goals are important.

- Explain how happiness comes from the pursuit of meaningful personal goals.

- Give clients some examples of goals and then help them brainstorm their own lifetime goals.

- Be accepting of their lifetime goals. Let them dream big!

Handout

Why Goals Are Important

. . . .

We only live once, and many people say that the most important thing in life is to do all that we can to reach our goals. Goals are important because they give us something to aspire to, drive our ambition, and foster self-esteem. We feel a sense of pride and joy when we reach our goals. And, perhaps most importantly, we will be happy with our life (and ourselves) in our elder years if we know that we reached our goals or gave it all we had.

Striving to be all that we can be is what ultimately makes us happy, and this process is something that psychologists call "self-actualization." We may not reach all of our goals, but we feel proud and content with ourselves when we know that we really gave it our best effort. Working towards your life goals is a great way to overcome depression and anxiety. So, let's get started!

There is an infinite list of goals, but here are a few examples to get you thinking about what you'd like to do with your life. Don't be afraid to dream big! "Going for the gusto" can really make a difference in your happiness.

- Make the varsity basketball team

- Be in the school play

- Make more friends

- Get a part-time job

- Go to college

- Learn to play the guitar

- Travel to Europe

- Be a nurse

- Get married and have kids

- Own a car

- Have your own house

- Have grandchildren

My Lifetime Goals

· ·

Make a list of the things you'd like to do with your life. What would you like to accomplish that you will be proud of in your old age? Don't be afraid to dream big!

1. _____

2. _____

3. _____

4. _____

5. _____

6. _____

7. _____

8. _____

9. _____

10. _____

Therapist Tips

Treatment Goals

- Explain the difference between treatment goals and lifetime goals.

- A lifetime goal is something clients want to achieve throughout the course of their lifetime.

- A treatment goal is something they want to achieve during the course of the treatment episode.

- Help your clients identify their personal treatment goals.

- Discuss what they would like to achieve from therapy or what they'd like to be different about themselves or their life.

Treatment Goals

· ·

Treatment goals are the things you want to accomplish through our meetings. They are specific goals that you can accomplish during the time we are working together in counseling. Let's identify your treatment goals. Some examples of treatment goals might include:

- Pass all of my subjects this semester

- Make a new friend

- Engage in no more self-harm behavior

My treatment goals:

1. _____

2. _____

3. _____

SMART Goals

- Explain to clients that in order to reach their treatment goals, it is important to ensure that their goals are SMART.

- Discuss what SMART goals are (e.g., specific, measurable, attainable, realistic, timely).

- Provide a hypothetical example of how to turn a broader treatment goal into a SMART goal.

- Help clients turn their own treatment goals into SMART goals by making sure their goals are relevant to treatment, measurable, and likely to be attained within the current treatment episode.

- To do so, help clients shape vaguely worded goals ("Pass the 10th grade") into a more specific SMART goal ("Get at least B's on my report card").

- This is hard for most young clients. Be patient and accepting of an approximation of a SMART goal. The SMART goal can always be modified as you go along.

Worksheet

SMART Goals

. . . .

A "SMART" goal is one that is specific, measurable, attainable, relevant, and timely. A SMART goal breaks down the treatment goal into small steps that you can work on to help you reach your treatment goal. Here are some questions to ask yourself when turning your treatment goal into a SMART goal:

- **S**pecific: What exactly do you want to accomplish?

- **M**easurable: How can you measure your progress? When will you know that you have achieved your goal?

- **A**ttainable: Do you have the tools or resources to achieve this goal? If not, can you obtain them?

- **R**elevant: Why is this goal important to you?

- **T**imely: What is the deadline for achieving this goal?

Here is an example of how you can turn a treatment goal into a SMART goal:

Treatment Goal	SMART Goal
Pass the 10th grade	1. Do not skip any school 2. Do all of my homework and assignments and hand in on time 3. Study 30 minutes for quizzes and 60 minutes for tests 4. Get extra help if needed 5. Pass all my exams

Now, let's practice turning your treatment goals into SMART goals!

Treatment Goal	SMART Goal
	1. 2. 3. 4. 5.
	1. 2. 3. 4. 5.

Therapist Tips

How to Reach My SMART Goals

- Identifying SMART goals is a necessary first step in effective goal setting, but it doesn't ensure that young clients will actually work to accomplish these goals.

- Chances are, your clients have had these SMART goals on their mind for some time but have not been able to reach them.

- Help motivate your clients to work on their SMART goals by asking them some strategic motivational questions.

- Help them identify the behaviors that they have tended to do in the past that made it harder for them to reach their SMART goals.

- Then, ask them to identify some new, alternative behaviors that would help them reach their SMART goals.

- Doing so will help them be honest with themselves about what they've done that hasn't helped and what they need to do to achieve their SMART goal.

Worksheet

How to Reach My SMART Goals

· ·

Although we all have goals, sometimes we behave in ways that make it more difficult to achieve these goals. For example, a kid may sincerely want to be on his school's soccer team, but he may lack confidence in his ability to play soccer. In turn, he doesn't actually practice the skills needed to make the team and comes up with a bunch of excuses to not try out. Although the kid may feel relieved in the short run, he'll probably feel worse about himself later on.

Describe some behaviors that you have done in the past that have made it hard for you to reach your SMART goals.

1. _____

2. _____

3. _____

4. _____

Now, identify some behaviors that you could do that would help you reach your SMART goals.

1. _____

2. _____

3. _____

4. _____

Exploring the Consequences of Anxiety and Depression

- Explain to clients that assessing the consequences of a problem can help them develop the motivation to overcome it.

- Help your clients identify the negative consequences of their anxiety and/or depression.

- Then, ask them to identify how their life would improve if they were to overcome their anxiety and/or depression.

- Emphasize the potential positive impact that making positive changes could produce.

Worksheet

Exploring the Consequences of Anxiety and Depression

. . . .

Use the following worksheet to identify how anxiety and depression have impacted your life, as well as how reaching your SMART goals would make things different.

What are the consequences of my anxiety or depression? How has it impacted ...

1. How I feel about myself? _____
    _____

2. My friendships? _____
    _____

3. My family? _____
    _____

4. My schoolwork? _____
    _____

5. My hobbies and interests? _____
    _____

If I reach my SMART goals ...

1. How will I feel about myself? _____
    _____

2. How will my life be different? _____
    _____

3. What will my parents think? _____
    _____

4. What will my friends think? _____
    _____

5. How will it affect my anxiety or depression? _____
    _____

Pros and Cons Analysis

- Counseling is a very challenging process. Doing a pros and cons analysis is a very respectful way to help motivate reluctant kids to engage in counseling.

- Help your clients identify the pros and cons of coming to counseling.

- Don't try to convince them that they "should" engage in counseling.

- Empathize with the challenges of engaging in counseling while also encouraging them to consider its potential benefits.

- Let them know that you understand and can accept their ambivalence.

- Help them clarify their commitment to treatment.

Worksheet

Pros and Cons Analysis

· ·

Determining whether or not you want to participate in counseling can be a difficult decision. Use the following worksheet to come up with some benefits of coming to counseling, as well as some potential downsides, to help guide your decision. After you've come up with some pros and cons, indicate whether or not you think it makes sense to move forward with treatment by marking the appropriate checkbox at the end of the worksheet.

Pros of Counseling	Cons of Counseling
1.	1.
2.	2.
3.	3.
4.	4.

☐ I'd be willing to try counseling for _____ to see if it helps.

☐ I'd like to come to counseling for as long as it takes to reach my SMART goals.

☐ I don't think I need any counseling right now and I'd like to discuss this with my parents.

Working Toward My Goals

- Explain to clients that they can improve the likelihood of reaching their goals by monitoring the specific actions and steps they have taken toward that goal.

- Encourage them to keep an active record of the specific behaviors they have done in order to reach their SMART goals, using the following monitoring sheet.

- Ask them to bring the monitoring sheet to the next session for review.

Worksheet

Working Toward My Goals

. . . .

It takes consistent effort to reach a goal. You have to stick with it and not give up. Keep a record of what you have done to reach your goal. See if you feel proud of yourself for the effort you've put in.

Date	My SMART Goal	What I Did to Reach My SMART Goal

CHAPTER FOUR

Mindfulness:
Calming the Emotional Brain to Utilize the Rational Mind

CBT has evolved substantially over the years, beginning with a "first wave" approach grounded within behaviorist principles of classical and operant conditioning and then moving to a "second wave" approach that recognized the role of cognition on emotions and behavior. Most recently, a "third wave" of CBT has emerged that focuses on the tenets of acceptance and mindfulness (Hayes et al., 2011; Teasdale & Williams, 2014). In contrast to first- and second-wave approaches, which focus on eliminating symptoms associated with dysfunction, third-wave approaches emphasize non-judgmental awareness and acceptance as vehicles for change. In particular, third-wave approaches believe that change results almost spontaneously from a process of mindful, non-judgmental awareness.

Teaching third-wave mindfulness skills early in the course of treatment can help your young clients learn to calm their "emotional brain" so that they can better access their "rational, problem-solving brain" and utilize traditional second-wave CBT interventions. The efficacy of these third-wave interventions is supported by recent advances in brain research, which have helped us understand the neuroscience of stress. We now know that both acute and chronic stress alters brain functioning in a way that contributes to anxiety and depression. In particular, kids who have experienced acute trauma, or who are exposed to ongoing trauma (e.g., repeated emotional and/or physical abuse), often develop an overly sensitive stress response system that puts them in state of constant hyperarousal. In turn, they can be easily triggered by even relatively mild stressors.

Importantly, recent research on mindfulness has shown that regular mindfulness practice is a good anecdote to these brain changes (Ireland, 2014). Simply put, mindfulness relaxes the limbic system (the brain's emotion regulation center), which allows the prefrontal cortex (the brain's rational thinking and problem-solving center) to function better. For kids with a hypersensitized stress response, calming the limbic system through mindfulness practice is an important first step of treatment, as it paves the way for them to subsequently engage in traditional first- and second-wave interventions.

Kids who learn and practice mindfulness skills can better regulate their emotions and subsequently learn to be better rational thinkers and problem solvers. However, it is often a challenge to teach mindfulness skills to children and adolescents, as well as to motivate them to practice these skills. Young people may hold negative stereotypes regarding mindfulness practices, and most kids are not aware of the neuroscience research that supports its efficacy. The tools in this chapter will help you teach mindfulness skills to your young clients in a manner they can understand and will want to use in their lives.

Amygdala Hijack and the Neuroscience of Stress

- Don't be afraid teach kids about the brain and the neuroscience of stress. Remember, knowledge is power, and it will improve the therapeutic alliance and increase the chances of a successful treatment outcome.

- Use the following two handouts to teach your clients about the limbic system (the brain's emotional control center) and the prefrontal cortex (the brain's rational thinking and problem-solving center).

- Explain the physiology of the autonomic nervous system and the fight-or-flight response.

- Explain that "amygdala hijack" refers to how the fight-or-flight system takes over ("is driving the bus") when we sense danger and how this system actually "hijacks" the brain's rational thinking and problem-solving functions.

- Don't be shy to use the term "amygdala hijack." Most kids will think this is a pretty cool term and will want to know what it means.

- You can teach this to a young child if you are willing to alter your language to fit their level of comprehension. Use simple terms to describe brain anatomy and physiology.

- Teach the neuroscience of stress and mindfulness to parents as well.

Brain Anatomy and Physiology

· ·

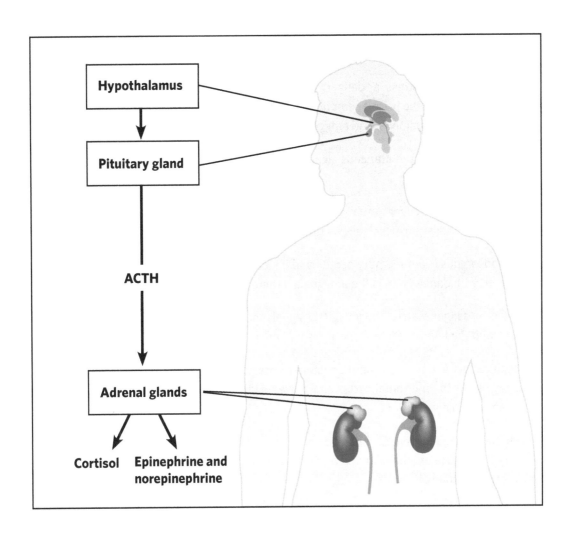

Amygdala Hijack and the Neuroscience of Stress

. . . .

1. When we experience stress, a "danger" signal is sent from the peripheral nerves (eyes, ears, etc.) to the limbic system, the brain's "emotional control" center, which includes the thalamus, hypothalamus, hippocampus, and amygdala.

2. The thalamus sends a simultaneous signal to the hippocampus and prefrontal cortex, the brain's "rational thinking" center.

3. In low to moderate "danger" situations, the prefrontal cortex rationally evaluates the situation and quiets the limbic system, which allows rational problem solving to occur.

4. The hippocampus is our memory center, and it stores all our memories, including any memories associated with danger. It tells the amygdala if there is a dangerous memory "match."

5. If there is a "danger match," the amygdala signals the adrenal gland to release adrenalin and cortisol, and the fight-or-flight response is initiated.

6. In a high danger situation, the limbic system reacts more quickly than the prefrontal cortex, which basically blocks the prefrontal cortex and prevents rational thinking from occurring. Hence the term "amygdala hijack."

7. During the "amygdala hijack," the hypothalamic-pituitary-adrenal axis (HPA) is stimulated, causing the release of adrenalin and cortisol, which activates the fight-or-flight system and leads to the stress response.

Therapist Tips

The Effects of Adrenalin and Cortisol on the Body

- Explain what adrenalin is and what its effects are when we are in fight-or-flight mode.

- Explain what cortisol is and what it does to our body during and after the fight-or-flight response.

- Compare our body's stress response to a car engine that is stuck in neutral with the engine racing at 100 mph.

- Ask the child what will likely happen to the car engine if it stays stuck at 100 mph and compare this to our body's chronic stress response.

The Effects of Adrenalin and Cortisol on the Body

· ·

Adrenaline increases your heart rate, elevates your blood pressure, pumps blood to muscles, heightens your senses, and boosts energy supplies. This is what is called "fight-or-flight" mode.

Adrenalin prepares you for "fight-or-flight" mode. Your body is all revved up when adrenalin is flowing, like a car with the engine going 100 mph.

Cortisol also helps you by slowing down some body functions to save energy for the fight-or-flight response.

For example, cortisol increases sugars in the bloodstream, enhances your brain's use of sugar, increases the availability of substances that repair tissues, alters the immune system responses, and slows down the digestive system, the reproductive system, and growth processes.

Adrenalin and cortisol help us when there is a real danger. However, chronic stress causes prolonged release of adrenalin and cortisol, which leads to some serious physical and emotional problems.

When kids experience a lot of stress, they develop a short fuse. Their fight-or-flight system goes off even when there is a low level of stress. Their adrenalin and cortisol also stay high so their body stays "revved up" nearly all the time (like a car that idles at 100 mph). Because of this, stressed-out kids overreact to small stuff and feel nervous or on edge nearly all the time.

Therapist Tips

Mindfulness Meditation and Brain Functioning

- Explain to clients that practicing mindfulness will help them regulate the fight-or-flight response and reduce stress reactions in their body.

- Emphasize how critical it is to calm the emotional brain so we can use our rational, problem-solving brain.

- Teach kids about mindfulness and how regular practice can "bring the car engine to a nice, quiet hum" where it should be.

Mindfulness Meditation and Brain Functioning

. . . .

Mindfulness meditation can help protect your brain against stress, and there's research to back this claim up. Research using functional MRI (fMRI) scans have shown that after an eight-week course of mindfulness meditation, the brain's fight-or-flight center (the limbic system) appears to shrink, while the "thinking" center (the prefrontal cortex) gets bigger.

What's more, this research found that the connections between the limbic system and the rest of the brain get weaker, while the connections with the prefrontal cortex get stronger. That means that the brain regions involved in the stress response can no longer "hijack" the rational, thinking part of the brain.

In a nutshell, what this research demonstrates is how useful mindfulness meditation practice is in helping us be calm, think rationally, and solve problems. The more we practice mindfulness, the better we can stay calm and solve problems without flying off the handle or getting so stressed out.

In other words, mindfulness meditation lowers the body's "engine" to a nice, quiet hum. Then, we can think and solve problems better.

You have to learn how to quiet the fight-or-flight response if you want to learn to manage stress and feel better, and mindfulness meditation is a way to do this.

Therapist Tips

Typical Stress Response vs. Desired Stress Response

- Describe how we typically respond to stress: We experience a trigger and we react to it.

- Contrast this with the desired stress response pattern, which involves processing and problem solving through the situation before responding.

- Giving a hypothetical example of a stress trigger (including how our response to that trigger can lead to different outcomes) can be helpful.

- Emphasize how mindfulness is the key to developing the desired stress response pattern.

Typical Stress Response vs. Desired Stress Response

· ·

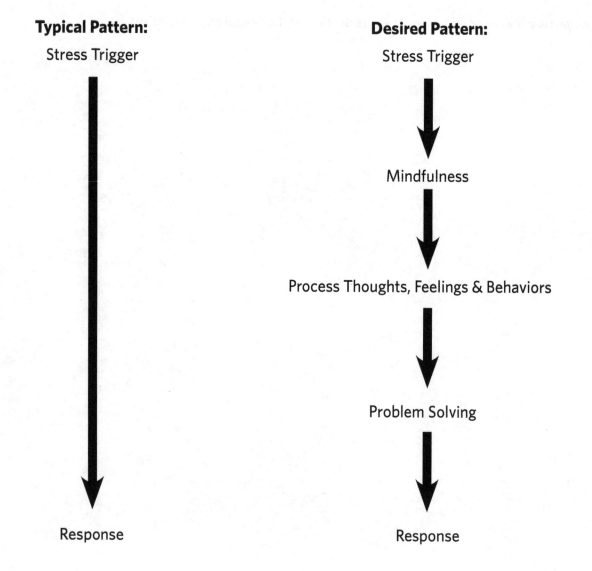

Typical Pattern:

Stress Trigger

Response

Desired Pattern:

Stress Trigger

Mindfulness

Process Thoughts, Feelings & Behaviors

Problem Solving

Response

Mindfulness Meditation

- Help kids understand what mindfulness means and remember to keep it simple.

- Simply stated, mindfulness means to be still and to focus on our present experience without judgment and without our mind wandering to the past or future.

- Explain how practicing mindfulness will help them manage their body's stress response and fight-or-flight system.

- Let them know there are many different ways to practice mindfulness and that you will help them find a way that suits them.

- Have them choose a mindfulness activity that they would like to practice with you in session, while encouraging them to keep experimenting at home to see what works best for them.

Mindfulness Meditation

. . . .

Mindfulness just involves focusing your attention to what is happening *right now*, instead of fretting about the past or worrying about the future. When you practice mindfulness, you are still and quiet, and you focus your mind on one thing in the present moment.

Mindfulness helps calm the mind and the body, which is important because when we are stressed, our mind is racing from all the adrenalin pumping through our body. And when our mind is racing, we can't control our emotions very well, think, or solve problems. So, we have to clear out all the clutter in our mind and focus on one thing to help calm everything down.

It is better to practice mindfulness meditation on a routine basis so you can learn to calm down and use your rational mind to solve problems.

There are lots of mindfulness meditation activities. You can do some traditional mindfulness activities, like deep breathing, pleasant imagery, and progressive muscle relaxation. You can also do some mindfulness activities that might be more fun, like listening to calming music, sucking on a piece of candy, blowing soap bubbles, or tossing a ball.

Handout

12 Mindfulness Activities for Kids

· ·

Here is a list of 12 different mindfulness meditation activities. Experiment with them until you find the one that is just right for you. Let's practice one right now!

Mindfulness Activity 1: Deep Breathing

- Recline or sit in a comfortable position with one hand on your diaphragm.

- Take a smooth, long breath through your nose for 3 seconds.

- Raise your diaphragm and fill your lungs to about 75% capacity.

- Hold the breath for 1 second.

- Exhale slowly through your mouth for 4 seconds.

- Pause for 1 second before taking your next breath.

- Maintain focus on your breathing.

- If your mind wanders, just refocus on your breathing.

- Continue for 5-10 minutes.

Mindfulness Activity 2: Pleasant Imagery

- Find a quiet place and sit or recline in a comfortable position.

- Close your eyes.

- Begin your deep breathing.

- Picture a pleasant place or scene in your mind (beach, waterfall, quiet stream, etc.).

- Picture all the details in your mind, like a movie camera moving slowly across a movie scene.

- Notice every little detail of the scene. What do you see?

- Notice the sounds and smells as well.

- Continue deep breathing while focusing on this scene in your mind for 5-10 minutes.

- Catch yourself if you lose focus and return to picturing the pleasant scene.

Mindfulness Activity 3: Progressive Muscle Relaxation

- Find a quiet place where you can be alone.

- Dim the lights, get into a relaxed position, and begin your deep breathing.

- Firmly squeeze both of your hands and make a fist.

- Make a fist as you inhale while deep breathing (3 seconds).

- Relax your fist as you exhale (4 seconds).

- Let your hands go completely limp and feel your hand muscles relax.

- Squeeze your eyes closed while breathing in, and relax them while exhaling.

- Repeat these same steps for your arms, shoulders, chest, legs and toes.

- Do this for 5-10 minutes.

Mindfulness Activity 4: Eating Candy

- Pick a piece of candy.

- Place the candy in your mouth, but do not chew or swallow the candy.

- Hold the candy in your mouth for 3 minutes.

- Be still and quiet.

- Focus on the flavor, texture, and all other aspects of the experience.

- Avoid the urge to chew and swallow.

- Concentrate on the moment. Tune out any distractions.

- Do not judge yourself or any part of your experience.

- Just observe and experience the moment.

- Refocus on the candy experience should your attention wander.

Mindfulness Activity 5: Music Observation

- Sit in a comfortable position.

- Close your eyes and begin your deep breathing.

- Play some quiet, soothing music. (Meditation music on "YouTube" and nature sounds – like waves, a babbling brook, or whale sounds – are all good.)

- Listen carefully to all the various sounds and instruments in the music for 5-10 minutes.

- Keep your mind focused on the music and all the different sounds.

- See if you can identify all the various instruments in the music.

- Catch yourself if your mind wanders and refocus on listening carefully to the music.

Mindfulness Activity 6: Soft Object Toss

- Use a soft, small-sized object (e.g., stuffed animal, nerf ball, tennis ball, and hackie-sack).

- Lie on your bed and toss the object up in the air as close to the ceiling as you can without the object touching the ceiling.

- Catch the soft object on the way down.

- Focus on making a good toss (as close to the ceiling as possible without touching the ceiling) and catching the object for 3-5 minutes.

- Don't be self-critical about any mistakes. Just keep doing your best.

- Keep your mind focused on tossing the object.

Mindfulness Activity 7: Mindful Snacking

- Obtain your parent's permission to do this mindfulness activity.

- Pick one of your favorite snacks (e.g., potato chips, ice cream, candy bar).

- Fix yourself a small portion of the snack (like a single serving bag of potato chips).

- Go to a quiet place by yourself.

- Take a small taste of your snack (e.g., one chip, one teaspoon of ice cream, one bite of candy bar).

- Close your eyes, breathe slowly and deeply.

- Savor the snack bite in your mouth for 30 seconds without swallowing.

- Experience the flavor and sensation of the snack in your mouth.

- Take another taste of your snack, and savor the flavor and sensation for 30 seconds.

- Repeat for 3 minutes or until your snack is gone.

Mindfulness Activity 8: Mindful Art Appreciation

- Find a photo, painting, or piece of art you really like.

- Go to a quiet place where you can be by yourself.

- Do some deep breathing.

- Look carefully at the photo, painting, or art piece.

- Notice all the details.

- Notice the colors, shapes, feel, and small details.

- Spend 5-10 minutes being mindful of all the details of the art piece.

Mindfulness Activity 9: Blowing Soap Bubbles

- Buy a bottle of soap bubbles.

- Lie on your bed and slowly blow a bubble into the air above you.

- Watch the bubble float up into the air.

- Breathe slowly and deeply while watching the bubble.

- Continue to blow bubbles and watch them float in the air above you.

- Notice how they move, fall, and collide with one another.

- Bring your mind back to noticing the bubbles if your mind wanders.

- Continue blowing bubbles for 5-10 minutes.

Mindfulness Activity 10: Gentle Stretching

- Stand with your feet at shoulder distance, with your arms by your side.

- Lift both arms straight over your head while breathing deeply.

- Stretch your arms up as high as you can and "reach for the stars."

- Hold for 10 seconds while breathing deeply and wiggle your fingers.

- Lean to your right, and touch your right hand on your right knee.

- Hold for 10 seconds while breathing deeply.

- Straighten up and then lean to your left, and touch your left hand to your left knee.

- Hold for 10 seconds while breathing deeply.

- Come back to a center position with your hands above your head.

- Bend forward and touch your hands to your ankles.

- Breathe deeply and hold for 10 seconds.

- Raise up to a center position with your arms above your head while breathing deeply.

- Bend backwards (not too much) with your arms and hands over your head and slightly behind you. Breathe deeply and hold for 10 seconds.

- Return to a center position, lower your arms to your sides, and breathe deeply for 10 seconds.

- Repeat for 5-10 minutes.

Mindfulness Activity 11: Observing and Describing a Comfort Object

- Hold a comfort object of your choosing (e.g., stuffed animal, pillow).

- Observe as many characteristics about the comfort object as you can.

- Don't observe just the obvious characteristics. Observe the subtle characteristics as well.

- Observe various parts of the comfort object, such as the feel and the smell.

- Hold and admire the comfort object.

- Snuggle the comfort object.

- Notice your feelings, thoughts, and sensations.

- Breathe deeply and hold the comfort object for 5-10 minutes.

Mindfulness Activity 12: Coloring

- Buy a coloring book or book of "mandalas."

- Color in the coloring book image or mandala.

- Focus on the coloring.

- Notice the colors, shapes, lines, and every detail.

- Keep your mind focused on the coloring.

- If your mind wanders, just come back to the coloring.

- Breathe deeply and smoothly as you color.

- Do this for 5-10 minutes.

Mindfulness Inquiry

- Conduct a "mindfulness inquiry" after clients participate in one of the previously listed mindfulness activities.

- Invite your clients to disclose what their experience was like by asking them, "What was that like for you?" or "Describe any part of your experience."

- There is no right or wrong answer. Validate whatever they disclose because this is their experience.

- Explore their mindfulness experience using all five senses.

- Encourage them to describe what emotional feelings they experienced, what physical sensations they felt, what thoughts went through their mind, and what they heard or smelled.

- Again, there is no right or wrong answer. The goal is to help them tune in to their experience in the present moment without judgment and be willing to share it with you.

- Provide verbal praise for their self-awareness and disclosure.

- After verbally discussing the experience, ask clients to write down their answers on the following worksheet.

Worksheet

Mindfulness Inquiry

. . . .

Use the following worksheet to describe what it was like to participate in the mindfulness activity. In as much detail as possible, describe what the experience was like, including what you felt, thought, heard, or smelled.

1. What was the mindfulness experience like for you? Describe any part of the experience.

    _____

    _____

2. What emotional feelings did you experience?

    _____

    _____

3. What physical sensations did you experience? What did you feel in your body?

    _____

    _____

4. What went through your mind? What thoughts did you have?

    _____

    _____

5. Did you smell anything?

    _____

    _____

6. What did you hear?

    _____

    _____

7. What was your body doing?

    _____

    _____

Therapist Tips

Mindfulness Monitoring

- Teach deep breathing with your clients in your office.

- Monitor their deep breathing and coach them as they practice doing it.

- Process the experience and ask them to describe what it was like them for. Validate their experience. (There is no right or wrong experience.)

- Ask them what percentage of time they could stay focused on the present moment as opposed to their mind wandering. Support their efforts at staying in the present moment.

- Ask them how calm they felt after the mindfulness exercise compared to how they felt before.

- Discuss how important it is to practice mindfulness. Emphasize that it's hard to use it when needed if they're not practicing it regularly.

- Invite your clients to do an "experiment" to see if regular mindfulness practice will be helpful.

- Encourage your clients to practice mindfulness at home three to four times per week for 5-15 minutes, depending on their age.

- Advise parents of the stress response and how regular mindfulness practice can ameliorate the stress response.

- Advise your clients and their parents that it is preferable to practice mindfulness in the child's bedroom or another quiet area of the home with few distractions.

- Have your clients (and/or their parents, depending on the child's age) use the "Mindfulness Monitoring" form to record their mindfulness practice at home.

- Have the parent monitor their child's mindfulness practice for compliance. This is especially important with young children.

- Invite the parent to do the mindfulness activity with their child to show support. (Parents can be just as stressed as their child, and they may benefit as well!)

Mindfulness Monitoring

. . . .

Use this monitoring form to record your mindfulness practice at home. Make a record of when you practiced mindfulness, what specific activity you did, how long you did the activity, and any thoughts, feelings, behaviors, or sensations that came up. Also make a note of what your stress level was like before and after the activity, as well as how much time you were able to keep a mindful focus.

	Date & Time	Mindfulness Activity	Duration of Mindfulness Activity	Stress Level Before Activity (0-10)*	% Time with Mindful Focus	Thoughts, Feelings, Sensations & Behaviors	Stress Level After Activity (0-10)*
Mon							
Tues							
Wed							
Thurs							
Fri							
Sat							
Sun							

*Stress Rating Scale: 0-1 = Little to no distress   5 = Moderately distressed and uncomfortable   10 = Extremely distressed

CHAPTER FIVE

Mood Monitoring:
How to Help Kids Be Aware of Their Feelings

In current society, we have all sorts of modern electronics and apps that help us monitor a variety of behaviors, including our daily exercise, heart rate, sleep, and food consumption – to name a few. In recent years, this trend has extended to the process of "mood monitoring" as well. Mood monitoring involves tracking our mood throughout the day to look for common patterns in how we feel, as well as to identify the factors that triggered us to feel this way. It has been well-established that "mood monitoring" can improve self-awareness and reduce depression and anxiety (O'Hara & Rehm, 1979).

This chapter provides you with a variety of activities that can help children and adolescents practice the skill of mood monitoring. To get clients into this habit, it is important to first educate them on the importance of self-awareness. When clients are better aware of how they are feeling, what they are doing, and what they are thinking, they can more effectively self-regulate.

In addition, it is important to help clients understand what feelings are and how they differ from behaviors. Part of this process involves working with clients to develop a feelings vocabulary so that they can begin to identify and label their feelings, including the life events that may trigger these feelings. Another component involves teaching clients that feelings fall along a continuum and helping them identify the intensity of their feelings. Once clients have worked to develop greater feeling awareness and expression, the use of daily and weekly mood monitoring logs can assist them in monitoring their moods on a regular basis.

The process of mood monitoring can have a powerful effect. It is not uncommon for even young children to develop spontaneous awareness of their feelings and how to better manage them through the use of mood monitoring.

Self-Awareness is Really Important

- Have some fun reading the story of the "ostrich with its head in the sand" on the following page.

- Emphasize how self-awareness is essential to our survival and good coping.

- Encourage your clients to be self-aware by "keeping their head up out of the sand."

- Discuss how CBT can help individuals become more self-aware of their thoughts, feelings, and behaviors – which, in turn, will help them to better manage their lives.

- I've been surprised that many kids have never seen a photo of an ostrich and don't know what an ostrich is, so I often find a photo on the Internet to show them. It's fun and helpful to do this.

Handout

Self-Awareness is Really Important

· ·

You know what an ostrich is, right? It's the largest bird in the world! It's really tall and has a very long neck. It has a big, round body, lots of feathers, and long, skinny legs. It's pretty funny looking, actually.

There is a popular story about the ostrich. The story is a myth, which means it's not really true, but it has an important meaning. It goes like this.

The ostrich is known for putting its head in the sand to look for bugs and seeds to eat. But, according to the myth, the ostrich puts its head in the sand to protect itself from danger. The ostrich feels safe with its head in the sand because it can't see any danger, like a wolf running to eat it. But, if you think about it, it isn't really safe just because it can't see danger.

Actually, the ostrich is in *more* danger because it is more likely to be eaten by the wolf if it isn't looking out for danger! Sticking your head in the sand actually makes you more at risk because you can't see the danger coming. How can you protect yourself if you are not looking around to see if there is any danger?

There is a famous saying that came out of this story: **"Don't stick your head in the sand!"** It's meant as a warning to keep your head up and look out for danger so you can protect yourself if necessary. You're not safe just because you "stick your head in the sand" and don't see any danger. You are actually more vulnerable with "your head in the sand."

Keeping your head up and looking around is called "self-awareness." As the myth teaches us, being self-aware is important to our safety and survival.

CBT encourages self-awareness so we can be safe, healthy, and well-functioning individuals. Self-awareness is the key to healthy psychological functioning. We want to be aware of how we are feeling, what we are doing, what we are thinking, and what is happening around us. If we have self-awareness, then we'll be much better able to manage life and whatever life throws at us.

We are going to be learning how to be self-aware in the next few CBT lessons. We'll begin with learning how to be aware of our feelings and then learn to be self-aware of our behaviors and thoughts. Let's get started.

What Are Feelings?

- Read the "What Are Feelings?" handout together with your clients.

- Describe how feelings are a subjective, internal experience that are different from behaviors.

- Emphasize that feelings are natural, okay, and helpful to us. They are not to be denied or ashamed of.

- Discuss how feelings are a signal of what's going on around us and help us manage what's happening to us in our life.

- Encourage clients to practice awareness and acceptance of their feelings without judgment or shame.

Handout

What Are Feelings?

. . . .

Feelings are different from behaviors. A behavior is something you *do*. A behavior is something that can be seen by other people, like laughing, talking, crying, hitting, and smiling. These are all behaviors that other people can see.

Feelings can't be seen by others. We experience feelings on the inside, such as sadness, happiness, fear, and anger. Sometimes, we see a feeling come out in a behavior. For example, when someone is sad (*feeling*), they might cry (*behavior*). However, we don't always see a feeling come out as a behavior because someone may feel sad but hide it and smile (*behavior*).

Feelings are neither good nor bad. They just are. It is not wrong to feel angry, sad, embarrassed, jealous, guilty, or any other feeling. Everyone has their own individual feelings. Feelings are okay and not to be ashamed of.

Feelings are very important. Like a traffic signal, feelings are a signal to help us navigate life. They help us figure things out. Feelings are like signals because they alert us to what is happening. If you are feeling scared, then it may mean that there is some danger. Feelings serve a positive purpose for us. Just like traffic signals, feelings are signals that we should pay attention to.

It is important for us to recognize our feelings and pay attention to them. If we pay attention to our feelings, then we can be aware of problems and solve them better. For example, if we are feeling afraid, then we can look around, see if there is any real danger, and then decide what to do. If we don't pay attention to our feelings, we will be like the ostrich with its head in the sand, and problems could get worse. Being aware of how you feel will help you solve problems and manage your life better. Let's practice.

Feeling Awareness Games

- The following activities are intended to help your clients develop greater self-awareness of their feelings in a fun and creative manner.

- Encourage clients to identify and express their feelings as they complete these feeling awareness games.

- Advise your clients that these games are not a "contest" but a way to develop a feelings vocabulary and improve feeling awareness.

- Model feeling awareness and how to spontaneously express feelings while engaging in role-play activities with your clients.

- Remember, it's okay to have some fun with these activities.

- For the Feeling Awareness Card Game, create a set of index cards with a different feeling word on each card.

Feeling Awareness Free-for-All

· ·

Let's see how many feelings you can name in 3 minutes. Just think of a feeling word and write it down. Don't worry about spelling!

1. _____
2. _____
3. _____
4. _____
5. _____
6. _____
7. _____
8. _____
9. _____
10. _____
11. _____
12. _____
13. _____
14. _____
15. _____
16. _____
17. _____
18. _____
19. _____
20. _____
21. _____
22. _____
23. _____
24. _____

Feeling Charades

· ·

Pick out one of the feelings listed below and act out whatever feeling you have chosen. The catch is: You cannot use any words. You can only use facial expressions, body language, and hand gestures – but no spoken language. Try not to be shy. Let yourself go and act out the feeling like no one is watching. Keep acting out the feeling until it is guessed correctly.

Sad

Happy

Mad

Excited

Tired

Energetic

Scared

Proud

Disappointed

Worried

Lonely

Restless

Bored

Confused

Feeling Awareness Card Game

· ·

Today we are going to play a game. I have a stack of cards, and on each card is the name of a feeling. We are going to take turns drawing a card from the deck.

When you pick a card:

1. Read the feeling aloud.

2. Role-play the feeling.

3. Describe a pretend situation when someone might have felt that way.

If you choose a blank card, pick any feeling you want and do steps 2 and 3.

Sample Feeling Awareness Cards

Sad	Happy
Mad	Excited
Scared	Embarrassed
Proud	

Therapist Tips

Feelings and Trigger Situations

- Use the following activity to help clients understand the relationship between trigger situations and feelings.

- Do not ask your clients to identify any personal situations for this activity.

- Instead, ask them to identify "pretend" trigger situations, as this is much less challenging. (Imagine if someone asked you to describe a trigger situation in which you felt "guilty." It would obviously be hard to share that kind of information!)

- At the same time, don't be surprised if clients start disclosing their personal triggers. It's quite likely that they will do this for some of the triggers. This is not a concern if it comes freely from them.

- Do not use this exercise to process any feelings or trigger situations. This is not the goal of the exercise. Remember, the goal is to simply help them understand the association between trigger situations and feelings, not to resolve any problematic feelings.

Feelings and Trigger Situations

. . . .

Feelings don't come from out of the blue. Feelings are triggered by a situation. Describe a **pretend** situation that might trigger someone to experience any of the feelings listed below.

1. Sad: _____

2. Angry: _____

3. Guilty: _____

4. Unloved: _____

5. Tired: _____

6. Anxious: _____

7. Happy: _____

8. Excited: _____

9. Disappointed: _____

10. Special: _____

11. Energetic: _____

12. Worried: _____

13. Lonely: _____

14. Restless: _____

15. Bored: _____

16. Confused: _____

17. Hopeless: _____

18. Proud: _____

19. Other (_____): _____

Therapist Tips

Subjective Units of Distress Scale (SUDS)

- Explain that feelings come in various levels of intensity. For example, anger falls along a continuum, ranging from mild irritation to extreme rage.

- In order for clients to become more aware of their feelings, explain that it is good practice not only to identify their feelings, but to identify the intensity of these feelings as well.

- Describe how we can use a simple 10-point scale to identify a feeling's intensity.

- We call this a "Subjective Units of Distress Scale" (SUDS) because it was originally intended as a measure of distress, but it can be used to identify the intensity of any feeling.

- Discuss that the direction of the scale is always the same. Higher ratings are associated with greater intensity, regardless of the feeling.

- Once clients have an understanding of SUDS, they can use the scale in conjunction with the mood monitoring activity that follows.

- You can also use the SUDS scale throughout the course of therapy to identify the intensity of your client's feelings, as well as their symptom level.

Subjective Units of Distress Scale (SUDS)

· · · · · · · · · · · · · · · · ·

The following scale helps you rate the intensity of your emotions. Use this scale to help you identify how strong your emotions are.

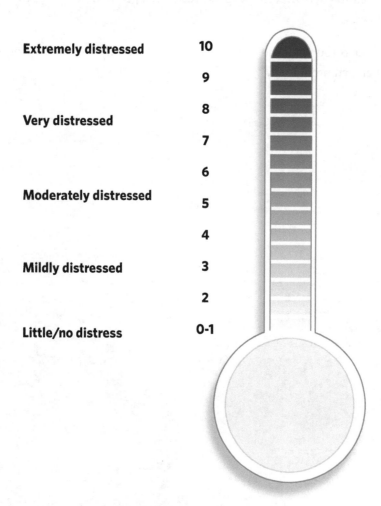

Extremely distressed   **10**

                                  9

Very distressed   **8**

                                  7

                                  6

Moderately distressed   **5**

                                  4

Mildly distressed   **3**

                                  2

Little/no distress   **0-1**

Therapist Tips

Daily and Weekly Mood Monitoring

- Help your clients understand that mood monitoring is a useful tool to help them better understand their emotions and what triggers them to feel certain ways.

- Mood monitoring is a very challenging task for most clients, so take your time helping young clients in particular. Your clients will be doing a great deal of self-reflection, which is likely to be quite challenging. It could take most of a session to identify a client's feelings for a typical day.

- Help your client practice this skill with you in session. Start with the "Daily Mood Monitoring" form and help them identify their moods and triggers for the current day or past 24 hours. It will be easier for them to remember this timeframe and get some practice with your guidance in session.

- Do not try to process or resolve any of your client's feelings while doing mood monitoring. The goal is simply self-awareness.

- Offer support and liberal praise for your client's efforts with mood monitoring. Do not try to relieve, "fix," or quell your client's distressful feelings. Rather, be sure to validate them and express empathy.

- Use the "Daily Mood Monitoring" form in session to help clients identify their feelings and trigger situations for a typical school day and weekend day as well.

- The "Weekly Mood Monitoring" form is less difficult to complete, as it asks clients to monitor their mood only three times a day, compared to every hour on the daily form. You can use your discretion as to what would be more helpful to your client, but I have found that it is more practical to use the weekly form as a learning activity to be completed in between sessions. It is also more likely to be completed by most kids this way.

- Urge your client to do weekly mood monitoring in between sessions, and ask them to track their moods at the end of the day before bed. This will take a lot of commitment and effort so it is often better to encourage the client to do this four to five days per week as opposed to daily monitoring.

- This is an example of a "collaborative experiment." When introducing the notion of mood monitoring, describe it as an "experiment" that clients can do in order to discover what triggers are associated with certain feelings.

- Advise parents of this learning activity and its relevance in treating depression and anxiety. Discuss how parents can support their child's efforts with mood monitoring in an age-appropriate manner.

Daily Mood Monitoring

· ·

Let's use the following chart to identify how you feel throughout the day. Looking back at each hour of the day, record whatever you felt and rate what the intensity of that feeling was (aka your "SUDS") on a 0-10 scale. In addition, identify what you were doing at each hour of the day, as that will help you identify what trigger situation(s) caused you to feel certain ways.

	Trigger Situation	Feelings	SUDS
7:00 am	*wake up for school*	*anxious*	*7/10*
7:00 am			
8:00 am			
9:00 am			
10:00 am			
11:00 am			
Noon			
1:00 pm			
2:00 pm			
3:00 pm			
4:00 pm			
5:00 pm			
6:00 pm			
7:00 pm			
8:00 pm			
9:00 pm			
10:00 pm			
11:00 pm – morning			

Worksheet

Weekly Mood Monitoring

· ·

Each night before going to sleep, use the following chart to identify how you felt in the morning, afternoon, and evening. Record whatever you were feeling during these times, and rate the intensity of that feeling (aka your "SUDS") on a 0-10 scale. In addition, identify what was going on at that time of day, as that will help you identify what trigger situation(s) caused you to feel certain ways. Some examples of how to fill out the chart are provided for you.

Time of Day	Monday	Tuesday	Wednesday	Thursday	Friday	Saturday	Sunday
Morning	*Anxious (7) Math test*						
Afternoon							*Happy (7) Watching football game on TV with family*
Evening							

CHAPTER SIX

Behavioral Activation:

Let's Get Active Again!

When kids get depressed or anxious, they often become lethargic, withdrawn, and socially isolated. They lose interest in participating in fun activities, even those that used to give them joy and pleasure in the past. All too often, they become overinvolved in video games and social media to the exclusion of healthy social and recreational involvement. However, this increased avoidance and isolation only serves to exacerbate their depression or anxiety.

Behavioral activation is an evidence-based intervention for depression that is designed to increase involvement in a broad range of healthy social and recreational activities (Gudmundsen et al., 2016; Tindall et al., 2017). It involves intentionally scheduling meaningful and reinforcing activities that improve mood. By increasing a client's engagement in these activities, they gradually decrease avoidance behaviors and become more active in participating in healthy, adaptive behaviors.

Importantly, the focus of behavioral activation is not only on scheduling activities that clients find pleasurable. Rather, it also involves scheduling activities that provide clients with a sense of mastery and are consistent with their values. While activities that are pleasurable may have transient effects on mood, activities that give clients a sense of meaning and accomplishment will help them build a life worth living, which serves to combat depression.

This chapter describes a variety of therapeutic activities that you can do with your young clients to help them become aware of their social withdrawal and identify healthy social and recreational activities that they value and want to engage in. However, for kids who are lethargic and depressed, behavioral activation is easier said than done. They may be able to identify some healthy behaviors with you in session but then fail to act on them in their life. Accordingly, this chapter also describes how you can identify and overcome the natural barriers that often prevent kids from engaging in healthy social and recreational activities.

What is Behavioral Activation?

- Begin with psychoeducation and a review of CBT theory as it pertains to behavioral activation.

- Remind your clients that thoughts, feelings, and behaviors are all interrelated, and what we do affects our mood.

- Discuss how depression and anxiety often lead people to withdraw socially because it feels better in the short run – even though it actually makes depression and anxiety worse in the long run.

- Explain how clients can improve their mood by engaging in healthy, pleasurable activities and that this is the goal of behavioral activation.

- Many kids will be quite ambivalent about behavioral activation, largely due to the fact that social withdrawal is negatively reinforcing. You may need to review their SMART goals and do some motivational interviewing to help motivate them.

- Clients may also balk at doing new behaviors due to legitimate barriers, such as money, transportation, parental support or self-confidence. Let them know you understand these barriers exist and that you will help them problem solve and overcome them.

What is Behavioral Activation?

• •

Let's look at the triangle below. Remember, we've talked about how you can change your feelings (mood) by changing your behavior or the way you are thinking about something. In this lesson, we're going to focus on changing your behavior to improve your mood.

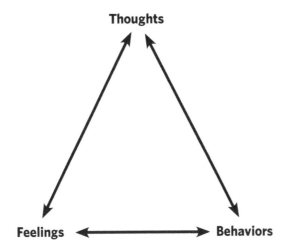

When kids get depressed or anxious, they often withdraw and lose interest in doing the fun activities they used to enjoy. They may drop out of a sports team or organization they used to participate in. They may stop hanging out with their friends. They may even start doing some unhealthy activities to try to feel better, such as using drugs and alcohol or going overboard with video games. While these behaviors may help them feel better in the short term, they make the depression and anxiety worse in the long term.

One way to fight depression or anxiety and start feeling better is to get more involved in healthy, enjoyable activities. For example, if you are feeling down, you can cheer yourself up by going to your team practice or being involved in a hobby or club activity. Or, you can just watch a funny movie. It really is possible to improve your mood by participating in a healthy behavior. This is one of the basic ideas of CBT, and we call it "behavioral activation." So, let's get active again!

Behavior Monitoring: Typical School and Weekend Day

- The following worksheets will help clients identify a baseline of their typical activities during school days, on the weekend, and for an entire week. It will also help them identify the feelings associated with each activity, as well as the intensity of those feelings using a SUDS rating.

- Develop a baseline of their routine activity level by helping your clients complete the "Typical School Day" and "Typical Weekend Day" behavior monitoring forms with you in session. This is likely to take a whole therapy session.

- Do not attempt to problem solve any apparent issues on their schedules. Just allow your clients to reveal themselves to you while being empathic and non-judgmental.

- Kids are often vulnerable to feeling judged when identifying their baseline behaviors because it is often quite apparent how significant their social withdrawal has become. They have likely had many battles with their parents over their social withdrawal and they probably anticipate a recapitulation of this with you.

- Be non-judgmental and empathize with the security that comes from withdrawing to a safe emotional zone while also reminding them of the potential benefit of doing behavioral activation.

- Once clients have identified a baseline of their typical school day and weekend schedule, invite them to do a "behavioral experiment" by monitoring their activities, mood, and SUDS ratings for an entire week to see what activities are associated with their moods. Use the "Weekly" behavior monitoring form for this exercise, which is abbreviated but more likely to be completed by clients between sessions than the daily form.

- Be mindful that your clients may identify a positive mood associated with social isolation due to the negative reinforcement associated with avoiding socially stressful situations. Help your clients understand this.

Behavior Monitoring: Typical School Day

· ·

Identify the activities that you do on a typical school day, as well as the feelings associated with these activities. Then, provide a SUDS rating (0-10) to describe the intensity of these feelings.

Time of Day	Activity	Feelings	SUDS
7:00 am			
8:00 am			
9:00 am			
10:00 am	Math Test	Anxious	8
11:00 am			
Noon			
1:00 pm			
2:00 pm			
3:00 pm			
4:00 pm			
5:00 pm			
6:00 pm			
7:00 pm			
8:00 pm – bedtime			
Bedtime to morning			

Behavior Monitoring: Typical Weekend Day

Identify the activities that you do on a typical weekend day, as well as the feelings associated with these activities. Then, provide a SUDS rating (0-10) to describe the intensity of these feelings.

Time of Day	Activity	Feelings	SUDS
7:00 am			
8:00 am			
9:00 am			
10:00 am	Wakeup	Bored	7
11:00 am			
Noon			
1:00 pm			
2:00 pm			
3:00 pm			
4:00 pm			
5:00 pm			
6:00 pm			
7:00 pm			
8:00 pm – bedtime			
Bedtime to morning			

Worksheet

Behavior Monitoring: Weekly

. . . .

Use the following chart to record the activities you do over the course of the next week. Use the SUDS scale to rate your mood (0-10) during each activity, as well as at the end of each day. Notice which activities are associated with negative moods, as well as which are associated with positive moods.

Time of Day	Monday	Tuesday	Wednesday	Thursday	Friday	Saturday	Sunday
Morning	*Math test (Anxious 8)*						
Afternoon							
Evening				*Swim practice (Happy 7)*			
SUDS for Day							

Review Your Behavior Monitoring Data

· ·

Look over your weekly behavior monitoring sheet and make a note of which activities were associated with a negative mood, as well as which were associated with a positive mood. Use the following worksheet to record your observations.

What behaviors were associated with a negative mood?

1. _____

2. _____

3. _____

4. _____

5. _____

6. _____

What behaviors were associated with a positive mood?

1. _____

2. _____

3. _____

4. _____

5. _____

6. _____

Life Values and Activities

- Help clients identify their personal values in the following five life areas: relationships, school/job, hobbies, wellness/spirituality, and daily responsibilities.

- What do they value (e.g., appreciate, like, hold dear) about each life area? What gets them excited or gives them zest? What is important to them and what gives them meaning?

- Help them identify up to three behaviors or activities that they might consider doing in these valued areas of life. Note that activities they "might consider doing" is an important phrase. This allows them to identify valued activities without necessarily making a commitment.

- Be mindful that clients will likely be unable to identify three activities in each life value area. Be accepting of their best effort to identify whatever is meaningful to them. It will likely take time and reflection to identify valued activities. Help them identify at least one to three valued activities. You can always add more if they identify some later in treatment.

- Explain that increased involvement in valued life areas will likely be a challenge in the short run, but it will likely help them feel better in the long run.

Life Values and Activities

· ·

Think about your values in each of the following five life areas. That is, what is important to you in these areas? What activity might help you feel excited and alive? Identify up to three activities that you might consider doing in each category to help you live in accordance with your values.

Life Areas	Activity 1	Activity 2	Activity 3
Relationships What's important to me: _____ _____			
School/Job What's important to me: _____ _____			
Hobbies What's important to me: _____ _____			
Wellness/Spirituality What's important to me: _____ _____			
Daily Responsibilities What's important to me: _____ _____			

Identifying and Overcoming Barriers to Healthy Activities

- Using their answers on the "Life Values and Activities" worksheet as a guide, help your clients prioritize and identify one to three valued activities that they'd *consider* doing.

- There are likely to be some barriers to doing these activities, including lack of time, money, transportation, or parental support – in addition to their own depression or anxiety.

- Help clients identify and problem solve any barriers involved in doing these activities.

- Discuss the potential benefits of engaging in these activities to improve their motivation so they are more likely to follow through with the activity.

Identifying and Overcoming Barriers to Healthy Activities

· ·

Oftentimes, there are challenges to doing a valued activity. Money might be tight or transportation is an issue. Sometimes, you may not have the self-confidence to do the activity. Work with your therapist to identify any barriers to doing the valued activity. Then, problem solve these barriers with your therapist. It might even help to discuss these barriers with your parents. Think of how things might improve if you actually do the activity. This might help motivate you to follow through with doing it.

Healthy Activity	What barriers make it difficult to do this activity?	What are some ways to problem solve these barriers?	What are the possible benefits of doing this activity?
1.			
2.			
3.			
4.			
5.			

Therapist Tips

Do a Behavioral Activation Experiment

- Help clients plan a healthy, valued activity that they can do in the near future.

- Ask your clients to monitor their SUDS ratings to see if doing the new, healthy behavior improves their mood.

- Involve the parents to help overcome any barriers and provide your clients with support. This is especially important with younger children.

- As children get into the habit of intentionally scheduling (and doing) healthy activities, discuss the pros and cons of gradually scheduling more of these valued activities throughout the week. There might be a benefit to scheduling more activities, but this could also be an overwhelming challenge for the child. Oftentimes, engaging in one to three new and healthy behaviors can be sufficient for significant improvement in mood. Therapist discretion is advised when considering adding further activities. Discuss this with your clients and pay attention to their needs and preferences.

Do a Behavioral Activation Experiment

· ·

Use the following chart to record the activities you do over the course of the next week. Use the SUDS scale to rate your mood (0-10) during each activity. In addition, do an experiment by planning a valued activity in the upcoming week. Make a note of your SUDS ratings after the activity and at the end of the day. Compare your SUDS ratings on this worksheet to the one you did previously. Does doing valued activities help improve your mood?

Time of Day	Monday	Tuesday	Wednesday	Thursday	Friday	Saturday	Sunday
Morning		Math test (SUDS = 8)					
Afternoon	Walk the dog after school (SUDS = 2)						
Evening	Study for math test (SUDS = 2)						
SUDS for Day	3-4						

CHAPTER SEVEN

Cognitive Processing:
Helping Kids Tune into Their Thoughts

You can safely assume that kids who are depressed or anxious are experiencing a lot of negative thinking. These thoughts are usually just under the surface out of conscious awareness, or what is commonly referred to as the "subconscious" mind. Our job as therapists is to help our young clients become aware of this negative thinking, evaluate it, and then change it into a more positive and realistic way of thinking (Brent et al., 2011).

However, before we can help our clients change their negative thinking patterns, they must first become aware of their thoughts to begin with. Therefore, as a general rule, cognitive processing precedes cognitive restructuring. Increasing self-awareness of thoughts is the initial goal. This is not an easy task, though, especially with younger children whose capacity for abstract cognitive thought is still developing. Reflecting on one's own thoughts is a metacognitive process, and the capacity for abstract thinking does not develop until mid-adolescence (Piaget, 1969). Indeed, not many adults think about their thoughts without considerable effort, much less adolescents or young children. However, my experience has taught me that adolescents and even young children can learn this skill if you teach it in a thoughtful and progressive manner, and through the use of developmentally appropriate, structured therapeutic activities.

This chapter contains a variety of therapeutic activities that are intended to help your clients become more aware of their thoughts in an open and non-judgmental manner. In particular, they will learn how negative self-talk leads to negative feelings and behaviors. They'll also learn about different types of negative thinking, or what I colloquially call "stinking thinking" (kids like this catchy phrase and remember it quite easily). In addition, they'll practice becoming aware of their stinking thinking, initially through hypothetical situations, and then in their own lives.

One final thought before proceeding. When going through the various activities in this chapter, it is important to keep in mind that the goal is simply to build self-awareness. The purpose of cognitive processing is not to change negative thoughts – although this sometimes happens spontaneously with awareness – but, rather, to help clients become aware of these thoughts so that cognitive restructuring can then follow, which is the focus of Chapter 8. While it can be tempting to try and reframe clients' cognitive distortions, resist the temptation to do so at this juncture, as doing so can increase resistance and hamper progress toward change.

Self-Talk and Stinking Thinking

- One way to help kids understand the concept of self-talk is through the analogy of a "thought bubble." Most kids, even very young ones, have seen a thought bubble in a cartoon and will readily grasp this concept. Take a moment to explain what thought bubbles are, including how they are used to reflect self-talk.

- Clarify how negative self-talk (aka "stinking thinking") leads to negative feelings and behaviors.

- Help your clients think of other hypothetical examples in which stinking thinking leads to negative feelings and behaviors. Don't press them to identify any personal examples just yet. This might be too much of a challenge. It will likely come naturally if you focus on educating your clients with hypothetical examples first.

- Do not try to correct any stinking thinking in the hypothetical examples. Doing so would be premature and likely cause anxiety and resistance.

- The goal of this handout is to understand that we all have stinking thinking when we are stressed and that the first step to managing it is to become aware of it.

Handout

Self-Talk and Stinking Thinking

Have you ever watched cartoons and noticed when there is a bubble placed above a cartoon character's head? Do you know what that bubble is supposed to represent? That's right, it represents the cartoon character's thoughts! The bubble reflects what the character is thinking but is probably not saying out loud. We call this "self-talk."

It's not just cartoon characters who engage in self-talk – everyone does! For example, have there ever been times when you've noticed that you are having a quiet conversation in the back of your mind? That's exactly what "self-talk" is. Self-talk is the stuff you say to yourself in your head but don't necessarily say out loud. Self-talk is perfectly normal.

Self-talk is important because the way you think affects how you feel and ultimately how you behave.

When kids are depressed or anxious, they tend to have a lot of negative self-talk, especially in stressful situations. This negative self-talk is called "stinking thinking."

For example, if you have a math test coming up and you are feeling nervous, you might be thinking, "I'm so lousy at math. I'll never pass this test." If you dwell on your stinking thinking, then you'll probably feel bummed, won't study much, and then do poorly on the test.

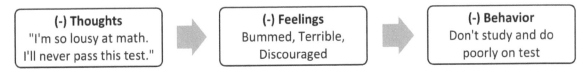

Can you think of any other examples?

Although stinking thinking may feel true in the moment, it is not usually accurate (and it certainly isn't helpful!). Stinking thinking only makes you feel bad about yourself, and it makes depression and anxiety worse. The first step in overcoming your depression or anxiety is to become more aware of your stinking thinking and how it is connected to your feelings and behaviors. We'll practice this important skill with the next several activities.

Different Types of Stinking Thinking

- Some older and more verbal teens might benefit from having a typology of stinking thinking. However, not everyone will need or benefit from this. Younger children will probably find it too abstract and likely won't relate well to this activity.

- Allow your teen time to process this typology. It's very complicated information and will take time to be understood.

- The goal is to encourage understanding and reflection, not personal disclosure.

- Be cautious about prompting for personal experiences prematurely.

Handout

Different Types of Stinking Thinking

· ·

When kids are depressed or anxious, they tend to see things in negative ways. It's like they are wearing "depression or anxiety glasses." Everything looks negative when you are wearing depression or anxiety glasses. Here are some of the different types of stinking thinking:

Catastrophizing: Catastrophizing is when one little thing goes wrong and you think it is the end of the world. For example, if someone does poorly on a quiz, then they think that they are going to fail the course, never graduate high school, and that their life will be ruined.

All-or-Nothing Thinking: When you think in all-or-nothing terms, you see things as either black or white. You are either a success or a failure, with no gray area in between. For example, someone might think, "I'm stupid because I didn't get high honors." There is no middle ground with all-or-nothing thinking.

Should, Must, Can't, and Won't: Depressed or anxious kids often have a lot of "shoulds, musts, can'ts, and won'ts" in their thinking. They "should" be the best; they "must" always be happy; they "can'ts" ever make a mistake; or they "won't" ever be wrong. Thinking in terms of "shoulds, musts, can'ts, and won'ts" puts a lot of pressure on you – and it only makes you feel more depressed or anxious when you can't live up to these standards.

Disqualifying the Positive: Depressed or anxious kids often disqualify the positive. That is, somebody might give them a compliment and they immediately disqualify, dismiss, or disprove it. For example, if someone says, "Nice goal in the game!" they might think, "Not really, the other team's goalie was terrible." Disqualifying the positive keeps you feeling miserable.

Mindreading: Mindreading is when you think that you know what someone is thinking without really knowing for sure. For example, someone with depression or anxiety might think, "I know she's going to say 'no' if I ask her to the dance." Or, "I know my teacher hates me." Mindreading is dangerous because you believe the other person is thinking something negative about you when they might not be.

Awfulizing: Awfulizing is when someone is almost always complaining about how "awful" everything is. They focus on the negatives and complain almost all the time. They hardly ever see any positives. When kids are awfulizing they might think, "This school sucks. The teachers and kids are all jerks." Awfulizing doesn't let you see the positives and keeps you depressed and anxious.

Identifying My Stinking Thinking

- Once kids have learned about the different types of stinking thinking, the next step is to identify the specific negative thoughts that they experience the most.

- In order to identify your clients' stinking thinking, provide them with a list of various negative thoughts and ask them to check which thoughts they've had.

- Kids will be much more likely to endorse and even self-disclose from a menu of negative thoughts – as opposed to being questioned about their negative thoughts in an unstructured discussion.

- It is quite likely that clients will check many of these negative thoughts.

- Be sure to praise your clients for being brave and acknowledging their stinking thinking.

- Don't leave them distressed with these negative thoughts that they don't have the skills to manage yet. Proceed to the next activity and provide them with some examples of positive alternatives.

Worksheet

Identifying My Stinking Thinking

· ·

You are probably having stinking thinking when you are depressed or anxious. Here are some common examples of stinking thinking. Check any thoughts that you have had. If there are other examples of stinking thinking you've had that aren't on the list, there's also a space for you to write them in at the end.

☐ I'm such a jerk.

☐ No one likes me.

☐ My life stinks.

☐ Nothing ever works out.

☐ It's hopeless.

☐ I'll never be happy.

☐ Everything is all messed up.

☐ It's too scary. I can't do that.

☐ I'm not good at anything.

☐ Everyone thinks I'm a jerk.

☐ I hate myself.

☐ I might as well give up.

☐ I might as well be dead.

☐ Other: _____

Identifying What Positive, Realistic Thoughts Look Like

- You don't want to leave your clients stewing with negative thoughts that were probably stirred up in the preceding exercise, so it's helpful to provide them with some examples of alternative positive thoughts.

- Your clients likely have a "blind spot" regarding positive thinking. They probably don't have a good idea of what a realistic, positive thought is like. They might have the idea that positive thinking is something Pollyannaish (e.g., "Oh, everything is just so wonderful!"), or they simply draw a blank about how to think in a rational, constructive manner.

- You are not telling your clients how to think. You are not implying that they should adopt these examples for themselves. You're simply giving some examples of positive thoughts that they probably wouldn't be able to think of themselves at this point.

- You are sowing some seeds for future self-directed positive thinking.

- Make sure to clarify that positive thinking is not Pollyannaish thinking. Positive thinking is both realistic and true.

Positive Thinking vs. Stinking Thinking

· ·

Here are some examples of positive thinking that represent an alternative to the stinking thinking examples from the previous worksheet.

Stinking Thinking	Positive Thinking
I'm such a jerk.	I am not a jerk. Sometimes I screw up, but who doesn't? I do some things okay.
No one likes me	Some people like me and some don't. But that's normal. You can't expect everyone to like you.
My life stinks.	I have some problems, but some things are okay. My whole life doesn't stink.
Nothing ever works out.	Some things don't work out so well, but some do. It's not all bad.
It's hopeless.	Just because I'm having a rough time now doesn't mean everything is hopeless. Things can work out if I work at fixing my problems.
I'll never be happy.	I may be bummed now, but I have my whole life ahead of me. I can find happiness if I work at solving my problems.
Everything is all messed up.	I have some problems, but some things are okay.
It's too scary. I can't do that.	I can do it if I stay calm, stay positive, and work at it little by little.
I'm not good at anything.	I'm not good at everything, but I am good at some things.
Everyone thinks I'm a jerk.	Some people might think I'm a jerk, but some other people respect me.
I can't handle that. It is too much for me.	I can do it if I stay calm and work hard.
I hate myself.	I'm not perfect, but who is? I have some good qualities.
I might as well give up.	I shouldn't just give up. I will keep on working hard until I get it right.
I might as well be dead.	This is not a good idea. Imagine how my family would feel! There is some reason for my life. I will carry on, and someday I'll be glad I did.

Pretend Stressful Situation: Stinking Thinking

- Once clients have learned about negative thinking, help them see how stinking thinking leads to unhelpful behaviors and distressful feelings.

- To do so, use the previous analogy of the "thought bubble" to represent stinking thinking, and ask clients to map out a hypothetical scenario in which negative thinking leads to upset feelings and unhelpful behaviors.

- Your clients will revisit this worksheet when you get to cognitive restructuring in Chapter 8, so you may need to prompt them to create a plausible scenario that depicts a situation with more positive evidence than negative evidence (e.g., a child who almost always gets good grades but is afraid of failing a test).

- It is important to have clients practice with a *hypothetical* scenario in this exercise, as opposed to asking them to focus on a personal experience. It will be much easier for them to identify stinking thinking in a hypothetical situation as opposed to a real-life situation of their own. You will probably ignite resistance and get a "deer in the headlights" look if you prompt them to discuss a personal trigger before they've practiced with a hypothetical one.

- Remember, the goal here is simply to reinforce how stinking thinking affects feelings and behaviors, which reinforces depression and anxiety. Avoid the temptation to challenge or reframe their stinking thinking, as doing so would be premature at this time.

Worksheet

Pretend Stressful Situation: Stinking Thinking

. . . .

Come up with a pretend stressful situation. Then, identify the stinking thinking, upset feelings, and unhelpful behaviors that someone would likely have in this situation.

Pretend Stressful Situation: _____

Stinking Thinking:

_____

_____

_____

_____

Upset Feelings:

_____

_____

_____

Unhelpful Behaviors:

_____

_____

_____

My Stressful Situation: Stinking Thinking

- Once clients have practiced with a hypothetical situation, invite them to identify a personal stressful situation and identify their stinking thinking, unhelpful coping behaviors, and upset feelings.

- It's best to ask clients to identify a low to moderate stressful situation (SUDS rating of 3-5), as opposed to a moderate to severe stressful situation (SUDS rating of 6-10).

- Remember: Do not try to change your clients' stinking thinking or negative coping behaviors at this point in treatment. The goal is for them to become self-aware and willing to disclose this to you without fear of judgment.

- Praise clients for recognizing and disclosing their stinking thinking, negative coping behaviors, and distressful feelings. This is a major accomplishment!

- Reassure your clients that you will teach them ways to develop positive thinking in the near future.

- This is a very challenging exercise. While most kids will tolerate the exercise quite well, it is possible that some will experience significant distress. If clients become distressed while disclosing their stinking thinking, have them do some grounding activities (e.g., deep breathing, pleasant imagery, etc.), or help them plan a positive social or recreational activity for later that day or evening. If necessary, review the "Positive Thinking vs. Stinking Thinking" handout presented earlier in the chapter.

My Stressful Situation: Stinking Thinking

· ·

Identify a stressful situation that has happened to you. Then, identify the stinking thinking, upset feelings, and unhelpful behaviors that you had in this situation.

My Stressful Situation: _____

Stinking Thinking:

_____

_____

_____

_____

Upset Feelings:

_____

_____

_____

_____

Unhelpful Behaviors:

_____

_____

_____

_____

Monitor My Stinking Thinking

- Invite your clients to practice being aware of their stinking thinking in their everyday life.

- Every day of the week, ask them to identify a stressful situation that occurred and to record their accompanying SUDS rating and stinking thinking.

- Remember: The goal is for clients to become aware of, but not to challenge, their stinking thinking.

- Sometimes, kids will come into session with some days left blank and say, "Nothing stressful happened to me that day." In this situation, advise your clients that we all experience stressful situations of variable severity every day and that it isn't necessary for them to only identify situations that were extremely stressful. A low or moderately stressful situation would suffice for this exercise (SUDS of 2-4).

Worksheet

Monitor My Stinking Thinking

· ·

Use the following chart to help you keep track of your own stinking thinking. Every day this week, write down something stressful that happens to you. It can be a situation that was just a little bit stressful, or something that felt totally overwhelming. Then, write down the stinking thinking you had about the situation, and record your upset feelings about the situation using a SUDS rating (0-10).

Day	Stressful Situation	My Stinking Thinking	SUDS Rating
Monday			
Tuesday			
Wednesday			
Thursday			
Friday			
Saturday			
Sunday			

CHAPTER EIGHT

Cognitive Restructuring:
Staying Positive Despite Challenges

Cognitive restructuring is at the heart of CBT, and it's virtually impossible to do successful treatment with depressed and anxious kids without helping them change their negative patterns of thinking (Friedberg & McClure, 2015). Generally, the process of cognitive restructuring involves identifying and replacing negative automatic thoughts with more positive, realistic thoughts. This is a challenging therapeutic task, and when working with kids, we want to teach this skill in gradual steps. This process first involves reminding kids of the CBT paradigm to emphasize how challenging their negative automatic thoughts is one way to help them feel better.

Another essential component of treatment involves teaching kids cognitive flexibility. In order to be able to push back on their stinking thinking, children must learn to understand that there is a great deal of ambiguity in life and that there are many possible interpretations to events. You can help kids develop this flexibility by teaching them to be a "thought detective," where they look for factual evidence for and against their stinking thinking. As always, it's important to initially help them practice being a thought detective with a hypothetical situation before asking them to apply this skill to their own trigger situations.

In order for cognitive restructuring to be effective, it must be done in a truly collaborative manner. As the therapist, you do not want to simply tell your client what the "right" way of thinking is. Although it can be tempting to provide the "right" answer when working with kids, it is important for them to come to this discovery on their own terms. These positive, realistic thoughts must come from the youth, not the therapist. In order to support kids in this process of self-discovery, it is essential to maintain a collaborative, "Socratic" posture throughout this delicate process. Failure to do so will only result in superficial benefit, or it will potentially alienate your young clients and undermine treatment.

Cognitive restructuring is a difficult task, but it can be done with the right set of tools. This chapter provides a variety of therapeutic activities to help kids challenge their negative thoughts and identify an alternative, positive way of viewing themselves, their life, and their future. The activities are designed to help kids through a process of "guided discovery" so that any change in their life view is genuine and self-determined. Importantly, the skills presented in this chapter incrementally build upon one other. A good therapist will be patient and respect the need for this gradual skill development process. While you may not be able to, or not need to do every one of these activities, skipping too many of these steps could create resistance and alienate your client from the therapy process.

What is Cognitive Restructuring?

- Begin by reviewing the CBT paradigm with your clients again, specifically as it pertains to cognitive restructuring.

- Emphasize the role of thoughts in contributing to depression and anxiety: Negative thinking is connected to negative behaviors and mood, whereas positive thinking is connected to feeling good and healthy behaviors.

- Discuss how changing stinking thinking into positive, realistic thoughts is one way to fight against depression and anxiety.

Handout

What is Cognitive Restructuring?

. . . .

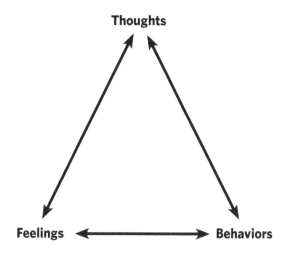

Remember our triangle and the basic idea of CBT? Yep, for every situation in life, we have thoughts and feelings, which influence our behaviors. In Chapter 6, we talked about how changing your behavior can improve your mood. In this section, we're going to focus on how changing your *thinking* can help you feel better.

Quite a long time ago, René Descartes, a famous French philosopher said, "I think, therefore I am." What Descartes was saying is that we are what we think. If we think negative thoughts, then we'll be a negative person. However, if we think positive thoughts, then we'll be a positive person. That means that you can feel better if you can change your stinking thinking into positive, realistic thinking. That is what cognitive restructuring is all about.

You've already learned how to become aware of your stinking thinking, so now it's time to learn how to turn this thinking around and develop some positive, realistic thinking instead. Let's practice!

Ambiguous Situations ... What's Really Going On?

- Cognitive flexibility, or the ability to see life from various perspectives, is an essential prerequisite for cognitive restructuring. This will help your clients get beyond their habit of rigid, narrow stinking thinking.

- Use the following handout to help clients develop the capacity for cognitive flexibility by discussing how many situations in life are ambiguous and open to various interpretations.

- After reviewing the handout, use the accompanying worksheet and ask your clients to think of at least three interpretations for each situation.

- They are likely to come up with at least one negative interpretation that is consistent with their depression or anxiety. It is critical that you validate the negative interpretation and not disqualify it.

- At the same time, remind clients that the examples on the worksheet are all ambiguous situations. Encourage them to identify at least two other interpretations for each scenario. Chances are they will come up with at least one benign or even positive interpretation.

Handout

Ambiguous Situations

. . . .

Lots of things in life are not exactly clear. Sometimes, we might not be sure what's really going on, or we might think we understand what is going on, but we could be wrong. These situations are called "ambiguous situations," and how we interpret ambiguous situations can have a big impact on our mood and behavior. Here's an example:

Let's say that a boy is sitting by himself at a cafeteria table. A bunch of kids at the table next to him are laughing, whispering, and looking over at him. The boy thinks that they are laughing at him and that they don't like him. He feels all bummed out – so he gets up, leaves the cafeteria, and doesn't talk to anyone the rest of the day.

However, the ending to this story could have turned out completely differently if the boy had interpreted the situation from another point of view. For example, let's say that the kids are laughing and whispering because they are talking about a teacher who they don't like, and they don't want anyone to overhear their conversation. If the boy sees the situation this way, then he'll probably feel fine, right? See how differently it could turn out depending on your interpretation of what is going on!

When kids are depressed and anxious, they tend to interpret things in negative ways, even when the situation isn't really negative. As you've learned, this is called stinking thinking, and it just makes depression and anxiety worse. To avoid getting into the trap of stinking thinking, it's important to check things out very carefully so you don't make the wrong interpretation of what is happening. Let's practice.

Ambiguous Situations ... What's Really Going On?

. . . .

There are lots of situations when it is not clear what is really happening. Read the following scenarios and think of **three** different explanations for what is happening.

Some kids are laughing and talking at a lunch table across from you. They are looking your way at times, laughing and whispering to one another. Suddenly, they get up and leave.

1. _____

2. _____

3. _____

At school, a kid is walking down the hall toward you. You say "hi" as the kid passes, but the kid doesn't say anything in response.

1. _____

2. _____

3. _____

You had a bad day at school. You just found out that you are doing poorly in one of your classes. Shortly after you get home, your mom asks to speak with you.

1. _____

2. _____

3. _____

You text a friend to see if he or she wants to get together and play video games. You wait two days and don't hear back from your friend.

1. _____

2. _____

3. _____

Thought Detective

- Introduce the concept of a "thought detective."

- Describe how a good police detective searches for factual evidence about a suspect's innocence or guilt before making an arrest.

- Discuss how unfair it would be for a police detective to make an arrest before having good factual evidence.

- Explain that this is what we need to do with our stinking thinking: We have to look at the factual evidence for and against our stinking thinking in order to make an accurate interpretation.

- Help your client practice this skill with the hypothetical example of the soccer goalie.

Thought Detective

. . . .

Remember, we've said that when teens are depressed or anxious, they often have stinking thinking. They often misinterpret things in negative ways, which makes them feel even worse. In order to help you think more realistically, one thing you can do is learn how to be a "thought detective."

Being a thought detective means that you make sure to get enough factual information to help you interpret a situation in an accurate manner. That way, you don't distort what is really happening. You have to ask questions like, "What's the evidence for thinking this way?" or "Is that really an accurate way to look at the situation?"

A good police detective goes out, asks questions, and gathers evidence to find out the facts. A police detective shouldn't arrest someone simply because he or she "feels" that the person is guilty. A police detective should only arrest someone when there is clear factual evidence of guilt. That's what you have to learn to do with your stinking thinking: check things out and gather the evidence for and against your stinking thinking. Examine the facts to see what is really accurate. Let's practice being a thought detective with the make-believe situation on the next page.

Soccer Goalie: Be a Thought Detective

· ·

The high school soccer team had a 7-1 record going into the championship game. The star goalie missed a save at the beginning of the second half, and the team ended up losing the game 4-2. After the game, the goalie was really bummed out. She was thinking that she blew the game and that she is a lousy goalie. She was worried that everyone was going to be mad at her, and she was thinking of quitting the team next year.

Now, be a good thought detective. What is the goalie's stinking thinking? What is the evidence that she's a lousy goalie? What is the evidence that she's a good goalie? What's not accurate about her stinking thinking? Based on the evidence, what would be a positive, realistic way for the goalie to think?

Situation	Goalie's Stinking Thinking	Evidence For the Stinking Thinking	Evidence Against the Stinking Thinking	Positive, Realistic Thinking
Star goalie misses a save in the beginning of the 2nd half of the championship game, and the team ends up losing the game 4-2.				

Practice Being a Thought Detective

- Once your clients have an understanding of what it means to be a thought detective, help them practice being one.

- Using the hypothetical scenario they came up with in Chapter 7 ("Pretend Stressful Situation: Stinking Thinking"), help them come up with some evidence for and against the stinking thinking.

- Let them know that there is almost always some evidence that supports the stinking thinking, but there is usually more evidence that contradicts it.

- Help clients analyze the evidence and determine a realistic, more constructive way to interpret the situation.

- Be cautious when using this intervention with a child who has experienced trauma or abuse. Cognitive restructuring is much more complicated with children who have been abused or traumatized. In these situations, it is recommended that you utilize evidence-based treatments for trauma and abuse (e.g., Cohen, Mannarino & Deblinger, 2016).

Practice Being a Thought Detective

Using the hypothetical scenario from the "Pretend Stressful Situation: Stinking Thinking" worksheet on page 107, practice being a thought detective. What is the evidence *for* this way of thinking? (There's usually some evidence for it.) In addition, what is the evidence *against* the stinking thinking? Based on the evidence, what is a realistic, positive way that someone could think about the situation?

Pretend Situation	Stinking Thinking	Evidence For the Stinking Thinking	Evidence Against the Stinking Thinking	Realistic, Positive Thinking

Stress in My Life

- Help your clients identify the stressors in their life.

- This is an important activity, as you will be asking clients to practice cognitive restructuring with one or more of these stressors in the upcoming exercise.

- In my experience, I have found that most kids will be quite compliant in identifying a number of stressful life situations from this list. However, be sure to ask if they have experienced any other stressors that are not included.

- Although some degree of distress is expected when completing this activity, most kids will tolerate this activity fairly well at this point in treatment.

- However, it is possible that this exercise could be overly triggering for some clients, so look for signs of excessive distress.

- If your client appears extremely distressed, practice a grounding exercise (e.g., deep breathing) and reassure them that you will help them resolve this issue as you proceed with therapy. In addition, brainstorm some positive activities that they could do after your session.

Worksheet

Stress in My Life

. . . .

Below is a list of stressful life events. Check any stressful events that you have experienced.

☐ Family problems (e.g., arguments/conflict with family members)

☐ School problems (e.g., low grades, school is too hard or stressful)

☐ Peer problems (e.g., few friends, peer bullying, conflicts with peers)

☐ Loss of a loved one (e.g., death or relocation)

☐ Past abuse (e.g., physical, verbal, or sexual abuse; parental neglect)

☐ Loss of a friend (e.g., moved away, ended our relationship)

☐ Break-up with a girlfriend or boyfriend

☐ Limited or no contact with a parent

☐ Drug or alcohol problem

☐ Arrest or legal problem

☐ Sexual problem

☐ Crime or violence in my neighborhood

☐ Performance/evaluation challenge (e.g., sports, tests, music performance)

☐ Traumatic experience (e.g., house fire, serious car accident, abuse)

☐ Parent mental health or drug/alcohol problem

☐ Other: _____

Challenging My Stinking Thinking

- In Part 1 of this activity, ask your clients to pick one of their stressful life events and map out the associated stinking thinking, upset feelings, and unhelpful behaviors.

- In Part 2, help them assess the evidence for and against their stinking thinking.

- Although there is usually more evidence that contradicts the stinking thinking, remember that there is usually some evidence to support it. It's important that you validate this.

- Resist any temptation to tell your client how they should think.

- Be Socratic. That is, ask probing questions to help them discover for themselves the evidence against their stinking thinking.

- Do not ask Socratic questions as if you are a lawyer interrogating a witness. Be supportive and genuinely curious about your clients' perceptions and life experiences.

- At the same time, remind them that their feelings, while legitimate in their own right, are not facts. Encourage them to look at the known facts of the situation. Use the facts and available evidence to help your client come to their own conclusion.

Challenging My Stinking Thinking: Part 1

· · · · · · · ·

Pick a stressful situation from your "Stress in My Life" checklist and describe your stinking thinking, upset feelings, and unhelpful behaviors.

My Stressful Situation: _____

Stinking Thinking:

_____

_____

_____

_____

Upset Feelings:

_____

_____

_____

Unhelpful Behaviors:

_____

_____

_____

Challenging My Stinking Thinking: Part 2

....

Using your real-life scenario from the "Challenging My Stinking Thinking: Part 1" worksheet, practice being a thought detective. Find the evidence for and against the stinking thinking. Based on the evidence, identify some realistic, positive thinking about the situation.

Stressful Situation	Stinking Thinking	Evidence For the Stinking Thinking	Evidence Against the Stinking Thinking	Realistic, Positive Thinking

Therapist Tips

My Stressful Situation: Positive Thinking

- Once clients have examined the evidence and identified more positive, realistic ways of thinking regarding their own stressful situation, have them identify how this new way of thinking can result in different feelings and behaviors.

- Help clients identify how this positive, realistic way of thinking would free them up to a whole new set of healthy behavioral options.

- Help them brainstorm some healthy coping skills they could practice based on their positive thinking. Some examples could include engaging in mindfulness, practicing a healthy behavior they identified in Chapter 6, or implementing a new coping skill altogether.

- Then, help them see how their feelings would change based on their positive thinking and behaviors.

My Stressful Situation: Positive Thinking

· ·

Now that you've identified more positive, realistic ways of thinking, let's see how changing your thinking can lead to different behaviors and feelings. How might you end up feeling with this different way of thinking? How might you be better able to engage in some healthy coping behaviors to better manage the stressful situation?

My Stressful Situation: _____

Realistic, Positive Thoughts:

_____

_____

_____

_____

Pleasant Feelings:

_____

_____

_____

_____

Healthy Behaviors:

_____

_____

_____

_____

Practice Positive Thinking

- Invite your clients to monitor their stinking thinking on a regular basis throughout the week.

- Encourage them to practice being a thought detective and to identify some alternative realistic, positive thinking.

- Describe this as an "experiment" to see how this might help them feel better.

- Remind your clients that positive thinking is not superficial or Pollyannaish. While positive thinking is generally more optimistic and constructive than stinking thinking, it is still realistic.

- Cognitive restructuring is a hard skill to learn, and it will probably take much practice and reinforcement with you over multiple sessions.

Practice Positive Thinking

. . . .

Practice catching your stinking thinking during the week and changing it into positive thinking.

Day	Stressful Situation	My Stinking Thinking	My Positive Thinking
Monday			
Tuesday			
Wednesday			
Thursday			
Friday			
Saturday			
Sunday			

CHAPTER NINE

Social Skills Training:
Teaching Essential Social Skills

Many kids with depression or anxiety problems have deficits in social skills (Albano & DiBartolo, 2007). They struggle with social relationships and develop avoidance patterns that lead to social isolation, which, in turn, exacerbates their symptoms. For some kids, these social skills deficits developed as a result of the depression or anxiety itself. These kids may have been quite socially competent to begin with but regressed socially as their depressive symptoms took hold, causing them to withdraw from previously enjoyed activities. Indeed, the negative thinking, lethargy, and anhedonia that accompany depression and anxiety make social engagement difficult. These kids are likely to recover their social skills as their symptoms improve throughout the course of CBT, and they may not need social skills training at all, or may only require some booster sessions.

However, other kids have social skills deficits that preceded their depression or anxiety – and that very likely contributed to it. These children have likely encountered social difficulties since toddlerhood, including difficulties with making friends, engaging in casual social interactions, being assertive, or engaging in productive problem solving. These kids will not spontaneously recover social skills from CBT because they never developed social competencies to begin with. Without social skills training, these kids will continue to have difficulties with social avoidance, so it is important that they receive social skills training as part of treatment for their depression or anxiety.

The activities in this chapter are designed to help your young clients develop competence with a set of essential social skills, including problem solving, assertiveness, and verbal and nonverbal communication. In particular, they will learn problem-solving skills to help them overcome difficult situations, as well as assertiveness skills to voice their needs in a healthy and productive manner. They will also learn how to improve their social skills by developing some essential social competencies in nonverbal and verbal communication, which will allow them to have positive interactions with adults and peers.

Problem Solving

- Kids with depression and anxiety often experience learned helplessness in the face of difficult situations (Seligman, 1996). That is, they don't believe there is a way out of their problems, so they just give up.

- However, there is a way out: They just have to learn how to be a good problem solver. Problem solving gives kids a practical and effective method to think outside of their depression or anxiety "box" and resolve a problem.

- Good problem solving consists of brainstorming options, thinking of the pros and cons of each option, and then picking the preferred option and trying it out.

- There are some sacrosanct ground rules to go over with your clients before teaching problem solving:

  Ground Rule #1: When brainstorming, there is no such thing as a bad option. Let your clients think outside the box. Do not try to control the brainstorming process, and do not critique or reject any option they come up with.

  Ground Rule #2: There is at least one pro and con for every option. Don't allow your clients to say there are no pros or cons to a certain option. There always is at least one pro and con.

  Ground Rule #3: Kids always get to choose their preferred option. This is a learning process for your clients. Trust the process and support them in making autonomous decisions.

- Help your clients implement their preferred option as an experiment and see how it goes.

- Repeat the process if the chosen solution is less than effective.

Worksheet

Problem Solving

. . . .

Use the following worksheet to problem solve a stressful situation that is going on in your life.

Identify a stressful problem in your life: _____

_____

What are some **options** to deal with this problem? (Tip: There's no such thing as a bad option when brainstorming.)

Option A: _____

Option B: _____

Option C: _____

What are the **pros** of each option? (Tip: There is always at least one pro for each option.)

Option A: _____

Option B: _____

Option C: _____

What are the **cons** of each option? (Tip: There is always at least one con for each option.)

Option A: _____

Option B: _____

Option C: _____

Think about your options, as well as their pros and cons, and pick the best option. (Tip: This is your problem and your life, so think carefully and make your best choice.)

Best Option: _____

Implement the best option and see how it works. Repeat the process if it doesn't work out as planned.

Being Assertive Can Help

- Describe how stressful it is to hold in your frustrations and that being assertive, if done appropriately, is perfectly acceptable.

- Help clients appreciate that being assertive can help them resolve problems and feel confident and proud (Sanchez, Lewinsohn, & Larson, 1980). Discuss how assertiveness is different from arguing or demanding.

- Review the steps involved in being assertive.

- Be sure to emphasize that there is no guarantee that clients will get what they ask for, even if they follow the assertiveness steps perfectly. Prepare clients for this possibility.

- Discuss the pros and cons of being assertive in real life, and assess the potential risks.

- Once you have reviewed the steps involved in being assertive, ask clients to develop an assertiveness plan to deal with a real-life stressful situation.

- Role-play the assertiveness steps for this stressful situation, and help your clients implement their assertiveness plan in the real world.

Handout

Being Assertive Can Help

· ·

Sometimes kids get stressed out because they don't know how to speak up for themselves. They might feel afraid to say how they feel or what they are thinking. They might be afraid to ask for what they need. They might worry that someone will be mad at them for speaking their mind. So, they hold their feelings in and become frustrated. This can contribute to depression and anxiety.

However, it is okay to express how you feel and to ask for what you need, so long as you do it politely. This is called "assertiveness." Being assertive is not an excuse to argue and demand things, and being assertive does not mean that you will get your way.

Assertiveness is an appropriate way to express your feelings and thoughts, and to ask for what you need. It is a healthy way to address a problem. However, there is no guarantee that you will get what you ask for, so you must be prepared to accept the answer you get. Whether or not you get what you ask for, you'll feel proud about standing up for yourself.

Here are the steps involved in being assertive:

1. Look at the person. Use a neutral, calm voice. Remain relaxed and breathe deeply.

2. Politely, describe what the situation is and how you're feeling about it:
    "I am feeling _____ about _____."

3. Politely, say what you think:
    "I am feeling this way because _____."

4. Politely, ask for what you need:
    "I need _____."

5. Listen to the other person's response.

6. Summarize the person's response back to him or her:
    "What you are saying is _____."

7. Do not argue if your request is not accepted.

8. Acknowledge the other person's viewpoint and accept it.

9. Thank the person for listening.

Practice Being Assertive

. . . .

Use this worksheet to develop an assertiveness plan to deal with a real-life stressful situation. Before you actually go ahead and implement your assertiveness plan, be sure to practice your plan with your therapist.

Think of a stressful situation that is going on in your life. Describe the situation below.

_____

_____

_____

Identify the person who you need to address the problem with. This is who you need to talk to.

_____

Now, follow the assertiveness steps on your handout. Write out what you would say to this person. Write how you feel, what you are thinking about the issue, and (most importantly) what you need or want.

_____

_____

_____

_____

_____

Finally, consider the pros and cons of being assertive. What are the risks? What would you do if the person got angry or vengeful? What could you do to protect yourself?

_____

_____

_____

Remember: You must accept the answer you receive and not argue back. You must always be respectful. You may not get what you ask for. However, if you follow these assertiveness steps, then you will feel proud of yourself, others will respect you, and you may feel less frustrated.

Communication Skills

- Discuss how good communication skills are essential for positive social relationships.

- Describe the difference between verbal communication and nonverbal communication.

- Describe how nonverbal communication skills are actually more important than verbal communication.

- Review the list of essential nonverbal communication skills, and give an example of each one.

- Emphasize how critical these relatively simple nonverbal skills are.

Communication Skills

. . . .

Communication is one of the most important social skills. All relationships – including the relationships you have with your parents, teachers, peers, and others – require good communication. You need to communicate well with others if you want to have good relationships.

What does communication mean? Communication involves not only **what** you say, but also **how** you say it. The "what you say" part is called "verbal communication" and the "how you say it" part is called "nonverbal communication."

We communicate with the words that we use and also through our tone of voice, facial expressions, and body language. For example, you could say "nice shirt" to someone, and it could have two very different meanings depending on how you say it. You could say it with a nasty tone of voice and a mean look on your face, and it would be a put-down. Or, you could say it with a positive tone of voice and a smile on your face, and it could be seen as a compliment.

It is well known that ***nonverbal communication is more important than verbal communication.*** That is, how we say something (our tone of voice, the look on our face, or our body language) is actually more important than what we actually say (the words we use). So, good communication involves having good nonverbal communication skills.

Good nonverbal communication skills will help you make friends and get along better with all sorts of people. Let's learn more about this important skill.

Handout

Nonverbal Communication Skills

· ·

Here is a list of the most important nonverbal communication skills. Using these nonverbal communication skills will really help you form positive relationships with all sorts of people.

1. **Smiling.** Smiling is one of the most important things you can do to make a positive impression on someone. People naturally like other people who smile! Do you know anyone with a natural smile?

2. **Positive Tone of Voice.** Speaking with a positive tone of voice really makes a big difference. Things that are said in a positive manner usually go over better.

3. **Eye Contact.** Making eye contact says that you are confident and that you care about the person. You don't want to stare, but you want to make some nice, warm eye contact.

4. **Personal Boundaries.** People usually like some personal space, but being too distant isn't good either. Standing about arm's length away from someone is usually an acceptable distance. Personal boundaries also relate to what you talk about. Gossiping is a violation of someone's personal boundary. People don't like someone who gossips.

Practicing Nonverbal Communication

- Help your clients practice using nonverbal communication skills in a role-play activity.

- Remind them that the same phrase can have two totally different meanings depending on how they say it.

- Ask them to say each phrase in two different ways. First, have them say the phrase with a negative tone of voice and nasty look on their face. Then, ask them to say the same exact phrase but with a pleasant tone of voice and pleasant look on their face.

- Punctuation is intentionally left off each phrase to allow clients to interpret each scenario in a positive or negative manner.

- Help them appreciate the difference between these two ways of saying something.

- As the therapist, it's a good idea for you to go first by role-playing examples of negative and positive communication. Don't be afraid to hype it up a bit. This will help your clients feel less inhibited and more willing to engage in the activity.

Worksheet

Practicing Nonverbal Communication

. . . .

The following is a list of some common sayings. These sayings can have very different meanings depending on your nonverbal communication. Let's practice your nonverbal communication skills by saying these phrases using different voice tones, facial expressions, and body language so the saying has different meanings. Remember, it's not **what** you say, but **how** you say it.

1. Nice shirt

2. Spaghetti for lunch, again

3. I've got swimming tomorrow

4. Good morning

5. I have to go now

6. See you later

7. You're such an idiot

8. Oh, it's snowing

9. Your parents bought a red car

10. I've got Mr. Jones for my math teacher again

Having a Conversation

- Many kids with depression and anxiety are afraid of having a conversation. They feel awkward and often avoid people due to fear of embarrassment. However, conversation skills can be broken down into specific steps, taught, and learned.

- Describe the steps to having a conversation, and give some examples of each step. However, be prepared to hear clients chuckle at your "old fashioned" communication style. It's better to help kids identify some examples of how their peers communicate, as this will probably be very different from what we could imagine. Their language style is preferred over ours. At the same time, the essential steps will remain the same despite the vernacular used.

- Once you are finished going over the communication steps, practice them with your clients by engaging in a role-play exercise.

Handout

Having a Conversation

· ·

Although it can sometimes be scary to have a conversation with someone, you can make this process easier by breaking it down into simple steps:

1. **Use an "ice-breaker"** to get the conversation going. Ice-breakers include a simple greeting.
   Hey, what's happening? How are you doing?

2. **Start with an easy topic to talk about.** People often start a conversation with a topic that is really easy to talk about, like the weather, sports, or school.
   How do you like all the snow lately?

3. **Don't start a conversation with anything critical or controversial.**
   Don't say things like: *Why are you wearing that goofy hat?*

4. **Find something you have in common.** Bring up a topic that you think the person is interested in. Or, better yet, a topic that you have in common. Listen for something the person says that is of interest to you as well.
   Did you see the football game on Sunday?
   Oh, so you saw that movie! I want to see that movie too. How did you like it?

5. **Be genuinely curious** about the other person. Take an interest in learning about him or her.
   How did you like that math test?
   How's the swim team doing?

6. **Use "active listening."** Take the time to focus on really understanding what the other person is saying. Let the person know you understand by summarizing what he or she has said. Be positive and supportive. Help the other person feel special, appreciated, and understood.
   Sorry you didn't make the team. You must be bummed. You're a really a good swimmer. Maybe you can practice over the summer and make the team next year!

7. **Be Positive!** Say positive things and don't put people down. Notice the other person's strengths and give genuine compliments.
   Great game last weekend! You played great! You're such a good athlete.

8. **Avoid drama.** Some people love to gossip, but talking about other people behind their back is disrespectful and often causes problems. It can lead to jealousy, rumors, and hurt people's feelings. It is best to avoid drama and those who revel in it.
   <u>Don't</u> say things like: *Billy is such a jerk, don't you think?*

9. A good conversation can be just a minute or two. But, it's important to **end the conversation politely.**
   "Hey, nice talking with you. I gotta go, but see you later!"

Now, let's practice having a conversation in a role-play activity.

Therapist Tips

Practice One of Your New Social Skills

- Help your clients pick one of the social skills discussed in this chapter to practice in real life.

- Remind clients that they must be willing to face their fears in order to conquer anxiety. At the same time, reassure them that they will be in charge of selecting an anxiety trigger they think they can manage and that they will learn to face their fears in a gradual manner.

- Be mindful to help them pick a social skill and life situation that they are likely to be successful with. It is critical that they experience some success with this activity and that they don't capitulate to their anxiety and give up. This will only reinforce their anxiety and sense of social incompetence.

- Have them provide a SUDS rating with respect to the distress they anticipate they will experience, as well as how difficult it would be to actually perform the skill. Pick a situation with a low to moderate SUDS rating (3-5).

- Help clients practice implementing the skill with you in session before they attempt to do so in real life. Be sure that they demonstrate a reasonable level of competence with the skill before they complete the learning activity.

- Discuss the pros and cons of using the skill, including any potential risks and a plan to manage those risks. Avoid any real-life situations that carry a considerable risk.

Using Social Skills in My Life

. . . .

Now that you've learned some important social skills, it's time to apply them in real life. Remember, you must learn to face your fears in order to conquer them. Think about the skills you just learned in this chapter and identify a situation in your life to which you could apply one of these skills. Be careful not to pick a situation that would be too challenging because you are just learning these skills, and I want you to be successful. Pick a low to moderate stressful situation (SUDS rating of 3-5). Be sure to practice using the skill with your therapist before you try it in real life.

Skill you'd like to practice: _____

Situation where you could use the skill: _____

Is this a relatively safe situation? What are pros and cons of applying the skill to this situation? What could go wrong? How would you handle it if something went wrong? _____

_____

_____

_____

Describe how you would use the skill in this situation (be specific): _____

_____

_____

_____

How did it go? Was the skill helpful? What did you learn? _____

_____

_____

_____

CHAPTER TEN

Anxiety Treatment and Exposure Therapy:

How to Face Your Fears

The negatively reinforcing value of avoidance is what maintains the vicious cycle of anxiety. When kids are afraid of or anxious about something, they avoid it, which makes the anxiety go away in the short term but makes it worse in the long run. For example, a child who is anxious in social situations might isolate from peers and avoid answering questions in class in order to make the anxiety "go away." However, over the long term, this prolonged avoidance only makes anxiety worse. It teaches the child that anxiety is in control, and it gives control over to the anxiety. Over time, that child might stop participating in school activities and social situations altogether. The only way to overcome anxiety is to face it head on, and that is what exposure therapy does.

Exposure therapy is to anxiety as cognitive restructuring is to depression (Kendall et al., 2017). That is, it is an essential ingredient of anxiety treatment. In exposure therapy, clients work to face the very things that they fear, instead of avoiding or escaping them. Most kids will understand that they need to face their fears in order to overcome them and will acknowledge that they have been avoiding doing so. However, even with this understanding, they will still be very reluctant to begin exposures because it is an intimidating task that they do not believe they can face with success.

In my experience, the best antidote to clients' trepidation is to reassure them that they will be in charge of this process and that you will not push them or "make" them do something they are not ready to do. I often make an analogy to someone who doesn't know how to swim. Imagine how anyone would react to being forced into a pool before knowing how to swim! Who wouldn't dig in and resist? However, a good swim instructor is not going to have students go into the deep end, or even the middle, of the pool until they have learned some essential swimming skills (e.g., how to float, holding one's breath under water) and are ready to do so. Similarly, it's important to reassure your clients that you will teach them your necessary skills to face their fears and that they will be in control of the process.

Exposures can be done in a variety of formats, including imaginal exposure (having clients imagine confronting their feared situation) or in-vivo exposure (having clients face their fear head-on in real life). When working with kids, it's helpful to start with imaginal exposure in order to get them into the habit of facing their fears, as well as to have them experience success in doing so. Once clients have successfully confronted their anxiety in their imagination, you can work with them to conduct therapist-assisted in-vivo exposures – which involves helping them confront a facsimile of their anxiety trigger in session with you – followed by exposures on their own in their real life. With younger children, it is often advisable to involve the parent(s) in this process to ensure that kids have the parental support needed to complete exposures outside of session. In addition, you want to reassure parents of their child's competence so they do not inadvertently continue to enable their child by "protecting" him or her from anxiety.

Treating anxiety with exposure therapy is a complicated process. However, if you follow the steps outlined in the chapter, you will be providing evidence-based treatment and have a good likelihood of success.

Anxiety Education: The Neuroscience of Anxiety and Mindfulness Meditation

- Review the "Anxiety Education" handout presented in Chapter 2. Remind clients of the negatively reinforcing value of avoidance and stinking thinking.

- Discuss that in order to overcome their anxiety, clients will need to learn to face their fears through gradual exposure therapy.

- Assure clients that they will be in control of the exposure pace.

- Reassure the client that they will be in charge of the exposure activities as long as they are making gradual progress.

- Review the "Amygdala Hijack and the Neuroscience of Stress" handout presented in Chapter 4.

- Remind clients that they need to calm their emotional brain in order to use their rational thinking brain to manage anxiety. Remind clients that practicing mindfulness is one way to accomplish this.

- Practice mindful deep breathing in session with your clients for 10-15 minutes, and process the experience using the "Mindfulness Inquiry" form described in Chapter 4.

- Review the "Mindfulness Activities" handout from Chapter 4, and help your clients identify a mindfulness method they want to practice.

- Help clients understand that they will need to practice their mindfulness skills on a routine basis to manage the anxiety they will inevitably experience during exposure therapy. Encourage them to practice a mindfulness skill of their choice three to four times per week for 10-15 minutes. Ask them to keep a record of their practice and experience using the "Mindfulness Inquiry" and "Mindfulness Monitoring" worksheets described in Chapter 4.

The Neuroscience of Anxiety and Mindfulness Meditation

• •

Remember what you learned in Chapters 2 and 4 about anxiety, the neuroscience of stress, and mindfulness meditation? Let's review this information again, as understanding this information will help you manage your anxiety.

You have to learn how to stay calm if you are going to face something scary, right? We have to calm the limbic system (our "emotional brain") so we can use the prefrontal cortex (our "rational thinking, problem-solving brain"). The best way to stay calm is to practice mindfulness activities, like mindful deep breathing.

Let's review the steps involved in deep breathing again and practice. This will help you manage your anxiety.

1. Recline or sit in a comfortable position with one hand on your diaphragm.

2. Take a smooth, long breath through your nose for 3 seconds.

3. Raise your diaphragm and fill your lungs to about 75% capacity.

4. Hold the breath for 1 second.

5. Exhale slowly through your mouth for 4 seconds.

6. Pause for 1 second before taking your next breath.

7. Maintain focus on your breathing.

8. If your mind wanders, just refocus on your breathing.

9. Continue for 5-10 minutes.

My Anxiety Triggers

- Use the list of common anxiety triggers to help your clients identify their anxiety triggers.

- Ask them to identify any unique anxiety triggers that are not on the list.

- Kids may struggle with this task because you are asking them to face their anxiety, which they have likely been avoiding. Given this, it's helpful to review your initial intake evaluation to get an idea of what anxiety problems they (or their parents) reported upon intake before starting this task. You may need to remind clients of this information if they balk at reporting or forget any anxiety triggers.

- Make sure to provide clients with liberal verbal praise for their ability to acknowledge their anxiety triggers. Their willingness to acknowledge their anxiety is their first exposure task. Praise them for their courage in facing their anxiety challenges.

My Anxiety Triggers

· ·

The following are some common trigger situations that make kids anxious. Put a checkmark by any triggers that make you feel anxious. If you have any other triggers that aren't included on the list, there are some spaces for you to add these as well.

Anxiety Triggers	Check if "yes"
School quiz or test	
Giving a presentation at school	
Eating in the cafeteria	
Socializing at school	
A school social event	
Going to sleep or waking up at night	
High places	
Being home alone	
Public performance	
Athletic performance	
Meeting new people	
When my parent is away	
Making mistakes	
Other:	
Other:	
Other:	
Other:	

Create an Anxiety Hierarchy

- Once clients have identified their anxiety triggers, ask them to provide a SUDS for each trigger.

- Then, help them rank order these triggers into a hierarchy based on their SUDS ratings.

- Rank order them from highest (most anxiety-provoking situation) to lowest (least anxiety-provoking situation).

- Next, help them select an anxiety trigger to work on. Remember, they are in charge of this decision. The general rule of thumb is to initially select a trigger with a low to moderate SUDS rating (3-5). However, there are some caveats:

  o Sometimes, clients may assign similar SUDS ratings to a variety of anxiety triggers. In this situation, help clients think though the pros and cons of selecting among the various relatively equally rated triggers, with a preference for those with a lower rating, and have them chose their desired trigger.

  o Alternatively, there may be times when clients want to work on an anxiety trigger that has a high SUDS rating, even though there are other triggers with lower ratings. In this situation, help clients understand that it is critical that they only "go into battle" against anxiety with a good likelihood of "winning." Advise clients that every time they go into battle and win, they get stronger and anxiety gets weaker. By the same token, if they go into battle and lose, then they get weaker and anxiety gets stronger. Therefore, they must pick their battles strategically and only fight those that they believe they are likely to win. Having explained this, though, a good therapist will stay true to their promise and allow clients to determine how they will face their fears. So, in the end, you need to respect your client's choice in this matter.

- Oftentimes, you'll need to help client clients break down their anxiety trigger situation into micro-exposure components. For example, they may have a fear of birds and you may need to make a secondary exposure hierarchy that breaks this single trigger situation down into smaller steps. This is quite common and necessary with many anxiety triggers, especially those with a high SUDS rating.

Create an Anxiety Hierarchy

· ·

Remember how we said that you can't fix an anxiety problem by avoiding it? The only way to fix an anxiety problem is by learning to face it. We said that we'd help you face these challenges gradually and that you'd be in control. To help you do this, you need to make an anxiety hierarchy. An anxiety hierarchy is basically a rating scale where you rank all of the things that make you anxious, from those that are least scary to those that are the scariest. This hierarchy will help you identify what anxiety triggers to work on first and which ones to tackle later.

Look at your "Anxiety Triggers" list and give each trigger a SUDS rating (1-10) to indicate how anxious you get in that situation. Then, rank all of your triggers on the following hierarchy, with those that are most anxiety-provoking at the top of the list and those that are least anxiety-provoking at the bottom.

Anxiety Trigger	SUDS Rating
1.	
2.	
3.	
4.	
5.	
6.	
7.	
8.	
9.	
10.	

"Catastrophic" Stinking Thinking

- Remind clients that kids who are anxious have stinking thinking just like kids with depression do.

- However, the stinking thinking is of a different quality with anxiety. Kids with anxiety often engage in catastrophic thinking: They imagine the worst possible outcome and believe that it will happen to them. For that reason, we'll use the term "catastrophic stinking thinking" with respect to anxiety.

- Use the following worksheet to help clients identify the catastrophic stinking thinking associated with a variety of hypothetical situations.

- Remember: It is much easier to start with these hypothetical situations as opposed to asking clients about their own anxiety and catastrophic thinking.

Catastrophic Stinking Thinking

· ·

Kids have "catastrophic" stinking thinking when they are anxious. That is, they think of the worst-case possible outcome when it comes to their feared situations. What might a kid's catastrophic stinking thinking be in these examples?

1. A teen is afraid of flying in an airplane.

   Catastrophic stinking thinking: _____

2. A child is afraid of spiders.

   Catastrophic stinking thinking: _____

3. A ball player is nervous when he/she is up to bat.

   Catastrophic stinking thinking: _____

4. A fifth grader is afraid he/she will fall over the railing at a scenic overlook.

   Catastrophic stinking thinking: _____

5. A first grader is afraid to get on the school bus.

   Catastrophic stinking thinking: _____

6. A seventh grader is afraid to ride the roller coaster.

   Catastrophic stinking thinking: _____

7. A teen is anxious about the SAT exam.

   Catastrophic stinking thinking: _____

8. A teen is afraid to ask someone on a date to the dance.

   Catastrophic stinking thinking: _____

9. A youngster is afraid of the dark and going to sleep.

   Catastrophic stinking thinking: _____

Therapist Tips

Pretend Anxiety Situation: Catastrophic Stinking Thinking

- Help clients see how catastrophic stinking thinking reinforces the cycle of avoidance and anxiety.

- To do so, ask clients to pick one of the hypothetical examples from the previous "Catastrophic Stinking Thinking" worksheet to use in this exercise.

- Then, ask clients to map out the youth's catastrophic stinking thinking, anxious feelings, and avoidance behaviors in the hypothetical situation.

- Avoid making comparisons with the client's own anxiety triggers and catastrophic stinking thinking just yet.

Pretend Anxiety Situation: Catastrophic Stinking Thinking

. . . .

Pick one of the pretend anxiety situations from the "Catastrophic Stinking Thinking" worksheet. Identify the catastrophic stinking thinking, anxiety feelings, and avoidance behaviors that the person would likely have in this situation.

Pretend Anxiety Situation: _____

Catastrophic Stinking Thinking:

_____

_____

_____

_____

Anxious Feelings:

_____

_____

_____

_____

Avoidance Behaviors:

_____

_____

_____

_____

Therapist Tips

Pretend Anxiety Situation: Be a Thought Detective

- Review the therapy techniques described in Chapters 7 and 8 regarding cognitive processing and restructuring.

- If you haven't already, teach your client about being a "thought detective" as described in Chapter 8.

- Practice being a thought detective by identifying the evidence for and against the catastrophic stinking thinking in the previous hypothetical situation.

- Remind clients that there is almost always some evidence that supports the stinking thinking, but there is usually more evidence against it.

- Based on the evidence, identify some rational thinking to push back on the catastrophic stinking thinking.

Pretend Anxiety Situation: Be a Thought Detective

Now, be a good thought detective. Find the evidence for and against the catastrophic stinking thinking for this pretend anxiety situation. Based on the evidence, identify more realistic, rational thoughts that the person could have about the situation.

Pretend Situation	Catastrophic Stinking Thinking	Evidence For the Catastrophic Stinking Thinking	Evidence Against the Catastrophic Stinking Thinking	Rational, Realistic Thinking

Therapist Tips

Using Social Skills to Help Manage My Anxiety

- Your clients will need more than positive thinking to fight their anxiety. Before doing exposure therapy, you will also need to help them develop specific behavioral competencies that they can use to manage their anxiety. Otherwise, you are asking them to jump in the pool without knowing how to swim.

- For this activity, help your clients identify one or more of the social skills they learned in Chapter 9 (e.g., problem solving, assertiveness, communication) and help them brainstorm how they can apply these skills to their anxiety problem.

- You want your clients to include these skills as part of their anxiety coping plan, which they will develop in an upcoming activity, as well as for use during exposure therapy.

Using Social Skills to Help Manage Anxiety

Earlier in treatment, you learned a bunch of social skills, including problem-solving, assertiveness, and communication skills. Now, let's think about how you could use one or more of these skills to help you manage your anxiety problem. Look over the following questions to see which social skills might help you manage your anxiety.

Problem Solving:

Can you use your problem-solving skills to think through your available options for dealing with your anxiety problem?

Would problem solving help you identify a helpful action to take?

If so, use the "Problem Solving" worksheet (page 135) to work through your anxiety trigger. Identify your options for dealing with this trigger, examine their pros and cons, and then select the best option to help you with this anxiety problem.

Assertiveness:

Do you need to be more assertive?

Could you use assertiveness to help you manage your anxiety?

Do you need to speak up for yourself in order to manage your anxiety better?

If so, use the "Practice Being Assertive" worksheet (page 138) and apply it to your anxiety problem.

Communication:

How are your communication skills?

Could you communicate better with your peers or with adults?

Could communication skills help you to better manage your anxiety?

If so, practice the communication skills on pages 141, 145-146, 148 with your therapist and use these to fight your anxiety problem.

Therapist Tips

Using Distraction to Fight Anxiety

- Distraction is a simple, but commonly used, tool to manage anxiety.

- For this activity, you want to help your clients understand what distraction is and how to use it. Although they probably have an intuitive sense of this skill, it is good practice to make it explicit.

- Give some examples of how people use distraction to manage anxiety. For example, I often disclose how when enduring a shot or getting my blood drawn, I look at some object on the provider's office wall to refocus my attention away from the needle while doing some deep breathing.

- Help clients understand that if they can distract themselves from the anxiety triggers they are hypersensitive to, then they can lower their body's stress response and find relief from anxiety.

Using Distraction to Fight Anxiety

• •

Before we go into battle against anxiety, there is one more tool to learn. It's a rather simple and common sense coping tool that eases anxiety. It's called **distraction**, and this is how it works.

Most people don't like getting shots or having blood drawn at the doctor's office, right? A lot of people use distraction as a tool to help them tolerate medical procedures, which are necessary at times. For example, people might distract themselves from the procedure by looking at something on the wall in the doctor's office (while taking some deep breaths). Or visualize a tranquil scene, like walking down a beach. In both examples, they are "distracting" themselves from the procedure. As a result, they hardly notice the needle prick and before they know it the procedure is over!

The following are some examples of distraction techniques:

- Practice deep breathing
- Imagine being in a safe place
- Play basketball in your back yard
- Count cracks in the floor, wall, or ceiling
- Chew a piece of gum or candy and focus on its taste and texture

- Refocus your attention to background noises (e.g., cars honking, birds chirping)
- Doodle
- Trace the outline of your hand with your opposite hand
- Sing a song to yourself in your head

Now, let's think of how you could use distraction with some of your anxiety triggers.

Identify one of your anxiety triggers: _____

What distraction techniques could you use to better manage this anxiety? _____

_____

Close your eyes and visualize yourself taking some deep breaths and using this distraction technique to help you manage your anxiety. Do you think this might help?

Make a "Game Plan" to Face Anxiety

- Explain how a sports team has a pre-season training camp to practice before the regular season.

- Explain that your clients have been in training camp and how they have learned all sorts of skills (e.g., "plays") to help them be successful facing their anxiety challenges.

- Explain that it is now time to develop a "game plan" to fight anxiety.

- Emphasize that every time they face their anxiety and win, they get stronger and their anxiety gets weaker.

- However, warn them that the opposite is also true. That is, if they go into battle against anxiety and anxiety wins, then anxiety gets stronger and they get weaker. Given this, it's really important that they have a good game plan to fight anxiety, and they shouldn't go into battle until they are really ready and have a good likelihood of winning.

- In Part 1 of this exercise, ask clients to map out a low to medium anxiety trigger (SUDS rating of 3-5) and identify the catastrophic stinking thinking, anxious feelings, and avoidance behaviors associated with the trigger.

- In Part 2, help clients be a thought detective by identifying the evidence for and against the catastrophic stinking thinking, as well as more rational, realistic thoughts.

- In Part 3, help them identify some specific behavioral coping skills (e.g., mindfulness, social skills, distraction) that they can add to their toolbox. Help them see how using these skills, in conjunction with more rational thinking, can help them overcome their anxiety. Put all of these tools together to come up with an "Anxiety Coping Plan."

Make a "Game Plan" to Face Anxiety: Part 1

• •

Pick a low to medium anxiety trigger (SUDS rating of 3-5) from your anxiety hierarchy and describe your catastrophic stinking thinking and anxious feelings about this trigger, as well as what behaviors you do in order to avoid this trigger.

My Anxiety Trigger: _____

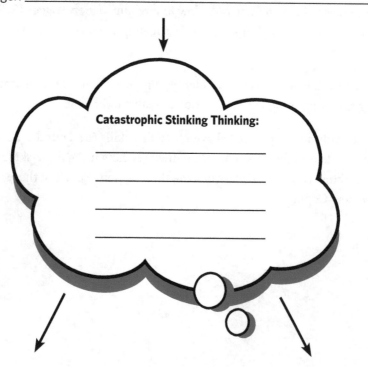

Catastrophic Stinking Thinking:

_____

_____

_____

_____

Anxious Feelings:

_____

_____

_____

_____

Avoidance Behaviors:

_____

_____

_____

_____

Make a "Game Plan" to Face Anxiety: Part 2

Now, be a good thought detective. Find the evidence for and against the catastrophic stinking thinking for your anxiety trigger. Based on the evidence, identify some more rational, realistic thoughts about the situation.

My Anxiety Trigger	My Catastrophic Stinking Thinking	Evidence For the Catastrophic Stinking Thinking	Evidence Against the Catastrophic Stinking Thinking	More Rational, Realistic Thinking

Make a "Game Plan" to Face Anxiety: Part 3
My Anxiety Coping Plan

. . . .

Now, let's use all your skills to develop an anxiety coping plan. Identify your rational, positive thinking about your anxiety situation. Then, identify some healthy behavioral coping strategies (e.g., mindfulness, social skills, distraction techniques) that you could use to fight your anxiety. Then, describe how you'll feel when you finally confront your anxiety and win!

My Anxiety Trigger: _____

Rational, Realistic Thoughts:

_____

_____

_____

_____

Pleasant Feelings:
Beating anxiety will make me feel better in the following ways:

1. _____

2. _____

3. _____

4. _____

Healthy Coping Behaviors:
I will use the following coping skills to confront my anxiety:

1. _____

2. _____

3. _____

4. _____

Imaginal Exposure:
Fighting Anxiety with My Imagination

- Help clients face their fears by initially having them confront their fear in their imagination.

- Explain that this is like a sports team having a pre-season game after training camp but before the real season.

- Ask them to close their eyes and take some deep breaths.

- Help them imagine, in as much detail as they can, being in the situation that is causing their anxiety.

- Ask them what their SUDS rating is at the beginning of the imaginal exposure.

- Prompt your clients to use their coping skills (positive thinking, mindfulness, social skills, and distraction) to fight their anxiety.

- Ask your clients to visualize themselves using these skills in as much detail as they can and to verbalize their coping skills to you as they are imagining themselves using them.

- Have them stay with the imaginal exposure for 20-30 minutes or until their SUDS rating is 3 or less.

- Advise clients that doing one imaginal exposure with you in your office will probably not be sufficient practice for the real "game," so they will need to practice in between sessions too. Encourage them to practice the imaginal exposure three to four times per week.

- For younger children, it's important to inform parents of the need for this between-session practice. Invite them to sit with their child and monitor the child's practice of imaginal exposures at home.

Imaginal Exposure: Fighting Anxiety with My Imagination

A sports team usually has some pre-season games before the real season begins. That's what we are going to do with imaginal exposure. We are going to have some pre-season games in your imagination before we go into a real battle against anxiety. To do so, we are going to practice confronting your fear in my office using your imagination. We'll practice using your anxiety "game plan" in your imagination and then decide together when you're ready for a real season game, okay?

1. Close your eyes and take some deep, slow breaths.

2. Imagine yourself in the anxious situation.

3. Describe this in as much detail as you can. What are you doing, thinking, and feeling?

4. What is your SUDS as you imagine this situation?

5. Now, start using your anxiety coping skills to manage the situation.

6. Imagine yourself using deep breathing or some other mindfulness skill.

7. Tell me how you are using these skills in your imagination.

8. Imagine yourself using your realistic, rational thinking. Say it out loud so I can hear it. Say it over a few times like you really mean it.

9. Now, imagine using any other coping skills you've learned that might help you in this situation, like assertiveness, problem solving, communication, or distraction.

10. Describe out loud what you're doing.

11. Imagine yourself using all your skills to fight your anxiety.

12. How are you doing? What is your SUDS rating now?

13. Keep fighting until your SUDS gets down to 3 or less and let me know.

Worksheet

Imaginal Exposure: Fighting Anxiety with My Imagination

. . . .

In order to be ready for the "game" against anxiety, you want to make sure that you continue to practice imaginal exposures outside of session. Try to practice your imaginal exposures 3-4 times a week, and use this log to record your practice. Each time you do an exposure, make a note of your SUDS rating before, during, and after the exposure. Remember to stay in the exposure for at least 20-30 minutes, or until your SUDS rating goes down until at least 3!

Date	SUDS		
	Before	**During**	**After**

In-Vivo Exposure:
Fighting My Anxiety in Real Life

- Before starting the in-vivo exposures, check in with clients to see if they want to make any changes to their anxiety coping plan since they have completed the imaginal exposure. Make any changes to the plan as needed.

- Explain to clients that in-vivo exposure involves two steps.

- The **first step** is a therapist-assisted in-vivo exposure, in which you help clients identify the best facsimile of the selected anxiety trigger situation that you can find in or around your office. You then guide them through the exposure with the facsimile trigger situation, either in or near your office, and help them use their anxiety coping plan to manage the exposure. I have done this with kids who have had a specific bird phobia, fear of making an oral presentation in class, athletic performance anxiety, and many others. You have to be willing to get a little bit out of your comfort zone, get up off your comfy chair, and be animated with your clients. But if you do, they will respect this and work with you.

- If the therapist-assisted in-vivo exposure goes well, then it's time to (finally!) move onto the **second step**: helping clients plan and do real life in-vivo exposures. Discuss their readiness for in-vivo exposure, and continue to practice or refine the coping plan if they are not ready. At the same time, be careful to not be complicit with their avoidance if they are balking excessively.

- Coordinate the in-vivo exposure with the parents of young children so they can help facilitate the exposure. Advise parents of the in-vivo plan so they are not taken by surprise and inadvertently abreact to the exposure. Help parents be supportive of their child without taking over.

- Have clients use the "In-Vivo Exposure: Fighting My Anxiety in Real Life" worksheet to record their in-vivo exposure experience. A SUDS of 3 or less is generally considered "resolved."

- Most of the time, kids only need to have one to two in-vivo exposure experiences that go well in order to gain competence in facing their anxiety trigger (and the majority of the time, exposures do go well if you follow this approach with fidelity).

- Once competence is apparent with the originally chosen anxiety trigger, you can move up the anxiety hierarchy and repeat the whole procedure with one to two more anxiety triggers.

- In my experience, you generally don't need to address more than two to three anxiety triggers on the anxiety hierarchy. Generalization often occurs once kids have been successful with a few anxiety triggers. At this point, they will often feel that the anxiety issues are largely resolved.

In-Vivo Exposure:
Fighting My Anxiety in Real Life

· ·

The battle against anxiety doesn't stop in the therapy session. In order to win the "game" against anxiety and come out victorious, it's important that you keep practicing in-vivo exposures at home, in school, or in your community. Use the following log to record your in-vivo exposure practice. Each time you do an exposure, make a note of your SUDS rating before, during, and after the exposure. Remember to stay in the exposure for at least 20-30 minutes, or until your SUDS rating goes down until at least 3!

Date	Exposure	SUDS		
		Before	During	After

CHAPTER ELEVEN

Special Topics in Treating Anxiety:
Applying Exposure Therapy to Specific Anxiety Problems

The exposure therapy procedures outlined in Chapter 10 are generic interventions that can be modified slightly for the treatment of specific types of anxiety disorders. In this chapter, I'll describe how you can apply the basic elements of exposure therapy to anxiety disorders that are common among children and adolescents, including social anxiety, separation anxiety, generalized anxiety disorder, and somatic symptom disorders. I have selected these disorders for further discussion because they are the more common ones that I have seen in my practice and, hopefully, will have application to your practice as well.

However, let me share one caveat. This chapter is not meant to be an exhaustive explanation of how to treat these conditions, as that would exceed the scope of this text. There are many subtypes and variations for each of these anxiety disorders that require unique treatment approaches. For example, the discussion of separation anxiety in the context of this chapter focuses on the specific subtype involving a young child who has not learned to sleep in his or her own bed and who is sleeping with the parents. There are many other clinical examples of separation anxiety disorder that are not addressed in this chapter, such as the child who has difficulty separating from parents and attending school, or the child who is fearful that some harm will befall his or her parents. While the generic approaches presented in Chapter 10, in combination those described in this chapter, could be applied to these other subtypes with some modification, I encourage you to complement the approaches presented here with other evidence-based treatment approaches for these anxiety disorders as described in the literature.

Social Anxiety

Social anxiety is one of the most common types of anxiety experienced among children and adolescents, and it is especially likely to co-occur with depression (Albano & DiBartolo, 2007). When kids have social anxiety, they primarily struggle to form relationships with peers, though they sometimes do with adults as well. They may have difficulty in performance situations, such as taking tests or taking part in an athletic competition, out of a fear of being judged negatively. In addition, they often lack fundamental social skills and struggle to say "hi" or engage in relatively simple, everyday conversation. These kids often avoid the cafeteria and eat lunch in the stairway, library, or counselor's office. They have few if any friends. They walk along the side of the school hallway, hoping to be ignored and left alone. They don't join any extracurricular activities, and they hibernate at home after school and on the weekends. In addition, they are likely to be overinvolved in social media as a vicarious means of socializing.

Social anxiety can lead to a self-fulfilling cycle, as kids who are worried about looking "foolish" or "embarrassing" themselves in social situations experience increased anxiety about that situation – which, in turn, can cause their actual or perceived performance to suffer. For example, kids who are scared of speaking in public may become so nervous when asked to give a class presentation that they stutter or clam up in front of their classmates. As a result, kids with social anxiety try to escape social situations or avoid them altogether, which brings short-term relief but only causes further social withdrawal and anxiety in the long run.

When working with kids with social anxiety, it is important to first help them develop the social skills described in Chapter 9 so they can engage in normal social interactions with competence and confidence. As I've described earlier, doing otherwise would be like asking them to jump in the deep end of the swimming pool before they know how to swim. Once they have developed some basic social skills, such as learning how to have a simple, brief conversation, they can benefit from exposure therapy as described in Chapter 10. The following are some specific tips for implementing exposure therapy for the treatment of social anxiety.

Therapist Tips

- Provide psychoeducation regarding anxiety as described in Chapter 2 and relate this to social anxiety. Help clients understand the neuroscience of stress, including the "amygdala hijack" and the fight-or-flight response, and how it contributes to their social anxiety.

- Help clients understand how practicing mindfulness will help them stay calm and be able to use social competencies to overcome their social anxiety.

- Review how avoidance, while understandable and yielding relief in the short run, will not benefit them in the long run.

- Discuss the notion of catastrophic stinking thinking as described in Chapter 10 and how it is applied to social anxiety. That is, how they likely overestimate the likelihood and significance of social rejection or the need to be "super cool" to make a friend.

- Help your clients learn some essential social skills as described in Chapter 9 to help them have the necessary competencies to manage social interactions successfully. I have found that it is most helpful to teach these kids about nonverbal communication skills and how to have a brief and successful conversation. Teaching these basic skills often serves as a catalyst: As kids start to experience some success and gain confidence after using the skills, they begin to naturally engage in more and more social activity.

- Discuss how exposure therapy is an essential component of conquering their social anxiety and that you will help them develop and practice coping skills before they face their social anxiety in real life.

- Use the approaches outlined in Chapter 10 to prepare clients for exposure therapy. Create a social anxiety hierarchy and help clients choose a low to moderate social anxiety trigger to work on. Develop a social anxiety "game plan" that involves both cognitive and behavioral coping strategies for their anxiety trigger.

- Practice their social anxiety game plan using imaginal exposure until they have sufficiently habituated to this type of exposure. Make sure to only begin in-vivo exposure when they are well-prepared and likely to be successful.

- Oftentimes, clients will only need to do in-vivo exposures with two to three social anxiety triggers. Once they experience success with a few exposures, their confidence grows and their skills tend to generalize to other social triggers.

Separation Anxiety

Many young children with anxiety are afraid to sleep in their own bed and gradually worm their way into their parent's bed, which soon becomes the norm. This behavior is a concern not only because it eventually interferes with everyone's sleep, but, more importantly, because the child doesn't learn how to soothe him or herself to sleep. The ability to self-soothe when distressed is an enormously important life skill, and children who do not learn this skill at a young age are more likely to struggle with other aspects of their life that require the ability to self-regulate and navigate challenges (e.g., taking a test in school, trying out for a team sport, etc.).

When this occurs, kids can develop separation anxiety, which is characterized by an excessive fear about being away from parents or other attachment figures. They may refuse to go to school or participate in other activities due to irrational fears about "bad things" happening to their parents when they are away (e.g., being kidnapped). As a result, they excessively "cling" to their parents and react with extreme distress in the face of situations that involve separation, or even the prospect of separation.

Treatment for separation anxiety utilizes an exposure therapy approach that is based in object relations theory, especially the process of "separation-individuation" as described by Margaret Mahler (Mahler et al., 2008). According to the theory, children between one and three years old learn to gradually separate from their parents as they develop the motor skills to crawl and walk. They become curious and use their newfound motor skills to leave the security of their parents and explore the world. They generally encounter some minor challenges (e.g., stumbling down a step or bumping into a cabinet) that cause some distress, which leads them to return to their parents for comfort, reassurance, and security. After being reassured by their parents, they experience renewed confidence and curiosity to explore the world again, and off they go only to encounter yet another inevitable minor stumble. In healthy development, this process of separating from the parents, exploring the world on their own, struggling, returning to their parents for safety and reassurance, and venturing off on their own again is repeated until the child gradually learns to be fairly secure on their own.

Children with separation anxiety – and particularly children who do not learn to sleep on their own – may not get the proper support they need from their parents when they encounter a challenge. Alternatively, their parents may be overprotective and not help them learn how to self-soothe and endure challenges on their own. As a result, these children don't learn how to persevere through normal challenges and don't develop the degree of resiliency needed for separation and autonomy.

When either of these situations develop, children feel insecure and anxious about separating from their parent (e.g., their safety object) and become excessively clingy. At night, they often become distressed after being left alone in bed and cry for help, or they go into their parent's bed. Parents become befuddled by their child's anxiety and neediness, causing them to overaccommodate the child's reassurance seeking by allowing the child to sleep in their bed (or by sleeping in the child's bed). As opposed to providing temporary reassurance and support needed for age-appropriate separation and autonomy, parents' excessive reassurance only serves to reinforce the child's anxiety. In these situations, it's important to realize that parents often have the best intentions for their child, but they are genuinely confused as to the appropriate response. The parent's accommodation is well-intentioned but misguided.

Mahler's theory behind the process of separation-individuation can be used to help children who have become accustomed to sleeping with their parent to learn to sleep on their own. The treatment process is a microcosm of the separation-individual process integrated with CBT exposure therapy. The treatment is conducted in the following manner.

Therapist Tips

- Provide anxiety psychoeducation to the parent and child as described in Chapter 2. Relate this to sleeping with the parent and the goal of the child learning to sleep on his or her own. Emphasize with the child and the parent how sleeping with the parent reinforces anxiety.

- Teach young clients deep breathing or some other mindfulness skill. This is essential as they will need a self-soothing skill to manage the distress they will most certainly experience when learning to sleep in their own bed. Have them practice a mindfulness skill with you in your office for 5-10 minutes and at home with parental monitoring three to four times per week for at least two weeks.

- Once they have learned how to use mindfulness to self-soothe, introduce the concept of catastrophic stinking thinking as described in Chapter 7. Help clients identify the catastrophic stinking thinking they have at bedtime when they are laying alone in their bed. Drawing pictures and using the "thought bubble," or doing a role-play exercise depicting this scene, is especially helpful with young children.

- Teach children to be a thought detective by examining the evidence for and against their stinking thinking as described in Chapter 8. These kids usually have fears about monsters, ghosts, or home intruders. You'll need to help them evaluate the reality of these notions. Having the parent's permission to address these beliefs is important, and having the parents discuss the reality of these beliefs with their child is also critical. In other words, have the parents echo your depiction of reality with respect to ghosts, monsters, and home intruders. Then, help children identify some realistic, positive thoughts about these issues and about going to sleep on their own in their own bed.

- Use the tools described in Chapter 10 to map out a "sleep coping plan" to manage their anxiety while falling asleep in their own bed. At a minimum, this strategy should include a mindfulness self-soothing skill and some realistic, rational thoughts to push back on their catastrophic stinking thinking. You may also want to teach them some distraction techniques. A "transitional object" is also quite helpful here, such as a stuffed animal or "blankie." Similarly, a soothing, time-limited music box or mobile can be helpful, but discourage any soothing objects that run continuously throughout the night (e.g., a TV), as these "safety objects" inhibit self-soothing and reinforce dependency on the external stimulus that can be hard to break.

- Teach parents about separation-individuation, but don't sound too esoteric. Make the description simple and related to the sleep problem. Then, explain this to the child. Again, use language that kids can understand, but don't underestimate their ability to comprehend this idea either.

- Once you have prepared your client and the parent(s) to begin the process of separation-individuation, use the following guidelines to begin the exposure therapy process. It is important to first have the child and parent engage in therapist-assisted in-vivo exposure, so the child can practice using mindfulness and positive thinking to self-soothe, and parents can practice their role as a transitional comfort object. I usually invite the parent and child to enact a bedside scenario and have the parent come in and out of my office and provide appropriate support and soothing to the child. We repeat this process two to three times as the parent and child would do at home.

- Do not initiate in-vivo exposures at home until the child has shown competence using skills to navigate the therapist-assisted in-vivo exposure. Then, plan to begin in-vivo exposures using the sleep coping plan you devised with the child and parent.

  o Ask the parent to sit on the side of the child's bed (with the child in bed) and do a soothing bedtime activity for 10 minutes to help lull the child to sleep (e.g., read a book, sing a lullaby, draw figure 8s on the child's back, etc.). It is also okay to use a nightlight or provide the child with a stuffed animal to hug, but remember to avoid external soothing objects that run continuously throughout the night or are excessively stimulating.

  o After 10 minutes, the parent should leave the child's bedroom but whisper in the child's ear that he or she will return in just five minutes. After a five-minute absence, the parent **MUST** return to the child's bedside and provide comfort to the child as previously described. The parent must not forget to return after five minutes or be late returning. This would severely compromise the child's trust in the parent's ability to offer reassurance and breed more anxiety. You may need to suggest that parents use a timer to alert them when five minutes is up.

  o After five minutes of being away from the child, the parent should return to the child's bedside and provide a second round of soothing and reassurance. However, this reassurance episode should be of shorter duration compared to the initial episode of bedside support. The second iteration of reassurance should be about five minutes.

  o After the second episode of reassurance, the parent withdraws again and whispers to the child that he or she will return in 10 minutes, a longer absence.

  o This process can be repeated with the time spent soothing the child being gradually reduced and the time the parent is away being gradually increased. Usually, two to three iterations of this process is sufficient for young children to fall asleep on their own.

- It is often helpful to provide children with a reward for successfully implementing their sleep coping plan. Doing so reinforces their ability to tolerate falling asleep and sleeping through the night in their own bed. A small reward the following day or a "smiley face" for a successful night can be accumulated and then exchanged for a larger reward. This will help motivate young children to comply with the procedure.

Generalized Anxiety Disorder and Chronic Worry

Many kids who struggle with anxiety have generalized anxiety disorder (GAD) or a tendency for chronic, obsessive worry. They often worry obsessively about some calamity occurring and require excessive reassurance, which does little to quell their anxiety. In addition, they obsess about the worry, which only further reinforces their worried state. Quite often, their obsession takes the form of perfectionism, which manifests as worries regarding academic grades or some other sort of performance achievement, such as athletics or artistic performance. Or, these kids may worry obsessively about the state of worldly affairs and Armageddon.

Treatment for excessive worry requires that children learn a set of coping skills to manage their worry without excessive obsession or reassurance seeking. Treatment for GAD within a CBT framework involves helping kids learn how to turn off their obsessive brain, engage in some productive problem solving, and resist the urge for excessive reassurance seeking. A number of the CBT techniques presented previously within this workbook are appropriate for GAD. For example, mindfulness skills can help children learn how to focus and control their mind. By practicing mindfulness, kids can learn how to ignore mental ruminations and focus on a single, soothing mental image. Problem solving is another useful tool that can address obsessive worry. Although children who worry obsessively may think they are engaging in problem solving, in reality they are just spinning their wheels and worrying about something in a very unproductive fashion. Teaching these kids problem-solving skills (see Chapter 9) can give them a tool for resolving a worry.

Finally, exposure therapy is a useful intervention that can help kids resist the need for excessive reassurance. Kids who worry often ask trusted others for reassurance regarding their worries, and they may also excessively search the Internet to find information to quell their anxiety. However, this excessive reassurance seeking only serves to further reinforce their worry. Even after being reassured, kids with GAD often think of some exception to the reassurance that was just offered, and are soon back again worrying and feeling the need for additional reassurance. Exposure therapy, which is discussed in the following Therapist Tips section, can help them reduce these reassurance-seeking behaviors by having them learn to resist the urge to obtain reassurance.

Therapist Tips

- Provide anxiety psychoeducation as described in Chapter 2 as it pertains to issues of chronic worry. Help clients understand how excessive reassurance seeking actually makes their obsessive worrying worse via negative reinforcement. Discuss how their catastrophic stinking thinking doesn't allow them to perceive the situation realistically and makes their worry worse, and discuss how a more realistic appraisal of the risks would be helpful. In addition, help them understand how learning to resist the urge for excessive reassurance via exposure therapy will help them resolve their excessive worry.

- Help your clients understand the importance of learning mindfulness to overcome their worry. Mindfulness can help ground clients to the present moment, as opposed to worrying about the future or fretting about the past. By practicing mindfulness on a regular basis, children can learn to let go of intrusive, worrisome thoughts instead of getting caught up in them. They can learn to refocus their thoughts onto a positive focus.

- Introduce cognitive processing and restructuring as described in Chapters 7 and 8 in order to help clients identify their catastrophic stinking thinking, evaluate it with facts, and develop more realistic, positive alternative thoughts that push back on their worried, catastrophic thoughts.

- It is critical that children learn how to use both mindfulness and cognitive restructuring techniques. These skills will alleviate their worry and help them manage the discomfort they will inevitably experience while they are learning to tolerate their worry without seeking excessive reassurance.

- Teach your clients how to express their worry in a healthy manner by compartmentalizing their excessive worries into a specific time slot. This can be achieved by helping children learn how to use a "worry journal" in which they can write about their worries but only at prescribed dates and times (e.g., Tuesday evening at 7:00 PM). The worry journal gives children an appropriate outlet for their worry while also teaching them to postpone and compartmentalize their worry. Children are allowed to discuss their worry journal with their parents, who can help the child problem solve or provide appropriate reassurance, but only at the prescribed date and time.

- In addition, teach your clients problem-solving skills as described in Chapter 9 to help them identify ways to resolve any problems that might underlie their worry. Problem solving can help them address their concerns in a productive manner, as opposed to worrying about a myriad of problems in a scattered, unstructured, and unproductive manner.

- Help your clients learn distraction skills as described in Chapter 10 to help them "switch channels" in their mind and focus on something other than their worry. You can integrate this with the principles of behavioral activation described in Chapter 6 in order to help clients become engaged in healthy, valued behaviors that would very likely occupy their mind and reduce their obsessive worry.

- Finally, use exposure therapy to help clients learn to resist the urge to engage in excessive reassurance seeking. First, help them develop a worry hierarchy that rank orders their various worries, and have them select a low to moderate worry topic they are willing to work on. Then, have them map out their unhealthy thoughts and the safety behaviors they typically do (e.g., excessive reassurance seeking).

- Next, help them develop a worry management plan that consists of cognitive coping skills (e.g., positive, realistic thinking they identified to push back on their catastrophic stinking thinking), as well as behavioral coping skills that they can use to calm themselves and resist the urge to seek reassurance (e.g., mindfulness, distraction, healthy alternative activity, worry journal, effective problem solving).

- Once they have a worry plan, help them practice the plan with imaginal exposures until they have developed sufficient mastery to enable successful in-vivo exposure therapy. The goal of exposure therapy is to gradually cut down the degree of excessive reassurance seeking they do, or the time they spend ruminating about their worries, to a reasonable level.

Somatic Symptom Disorder

Anxious children and teens often manifest their anxiety through a variety of somatic complaints, which can take the form of headaches, stomachaches or other gastrointestinal distress, or even obscure muscle aches and pains (Levy et al., 2011). Kids can become quite preoccupied with these somatic problems, causing them to withdraw from routine healthy activities and retreat to a place of perceived safety (usually their home or the nurse's office at school) because of their discomfort. Although withdrawing helps them feel better in the short term, it only exacerbates the avoidance and makes anxiety and somatic problems worse in the long run.

It is important to note that the somatic symptoms that these children experience are not imaginary. Rather, these children are hypersensitive to physical sensations – such as stomach sounds, minor aches and pains, and other body processes – which reinforces their somatic preoccupation. In turn, they overreact to symptoms that represent normal body processes or that reflect mild discomfort but are not indicative of a more serious medical issue. In addition, chronically elevated cortisol likely contributes to their gastrointestinal distress. As a result, they may engage in a variety of unproductive "safety behaviors" (e.g., obsessively altering their diet to quell their gastrointestinal distress, attempting to eliminate environmental sounds they think might precipitate a headache) in an attempt to manage their somatic discomfort.

Treatment for somatic symptom disorders involves helping clients become aware of their physical cues and safety behaviors, and encouraging them to use healthier strategies to cope with their somatic problems (e.g., mindfulness, distraction, acceptance, reframing catastrophic thoughts). The goal is for clients to persevere with their life and not let their preoccupation with their physical distress take control of their life. Although exposure therapy can help kids learn to tolerate their discomfort and remain actively involved in routine activities, it is important that they learn skills to tolerate their discomfort prior to engaging in exposures. The following are some specific treatment tips to guide this process.

Therapist Tips

- Before beginning treatment, care must be taken to have children's somatic complaints thoroughly evaluated by a physician to rule out any possible underlying medical cause. Once a medical cause has been reliably ruled out, you can proceed with confidence to address these concerns from a psychological perspective.

- It is helpful to assure clients that you understand their pain is real. Reassure them that their pain is not made up or "in their head." However, in the absence of any known medical cause, let them know that you can help them manage their somatic problems from a psychological perspective.

- Provide psychoeducation regarding anxiety as described in Chapter 2. Educate them about the role that chronically elevated levels of cortisol plays in creating various physical ailments, especially gastro-intestinal distress. Emphasize how avoiding activities due to their pain, while relieving discomfort in the short run, reinforces their somatic discomfort in the long run. In addition, explain how their catastrophic stinking thinking needs to be re-evaluated and replaced with a more rational and helpful reappraisal of their discomfort and the consequences of such. Help them understand how exposure therapy will help them persevere through mild to moderate discomfort so they can participate in various activities despite their discomfort.

- Help your clients learn and practice mindfulness to help them tolerate mild to moderate somatic discomfort. Deep breathing can be especially helpful with somatic complaints, as it helps them focus their attention on a soothing stimulus (e.g., their breathing) and away from their somatic discomfort. Deep breathing will also help them tolerate, or even alleviate, mild to moderate physical pain.

- Teach clients cognitive processing and restructuring skills to help them identify and push back on their catastrophic stinking thinking and maintain a positive mindset despite their discomfort. Help them develop a reasonable appraisal of their discomfort, as well as the consequences of avoidance versus the potential benefit of persevering and participating in activities despite some discomfort.

- Help clients understand that their somatic problems could be a manifestation of underlying anxiety and chronically elevated levels of cortisol. Let them know that this happens quite often to people. Use some well-known colloquial sayings to demonstrate this, such as, "What a pain in the neck Suzie has been lately" or "My head was pounding when the teacher was going so fast in math class." Help them identify some anxiety triggers (other than their somatic problems) in their life and develop a coping plan for these underlying stressors.

- It is often helpful to teach clients some distraction techniques as described in Chapter 10 to help reduce their perseverative focus on their somatic problem.

- Ask your clients to keep a somatic journal, in which they can write down their somatic complaints at a specific day and time each week (e.g., Saturday 10:00 AM). This will help them compartmentalize their somatic preoccupation while giving them an appropriate outlet to express their concerns. Children can share their somatic journal with a parent or healthcare provider (e.g., school nurse) to problem solve their somatic concern or obtain reassurance, but only at a prescribed date and time.

- It can also be helpful to teach your clients the notion of acceptance. Help them understand that they may not be able to change or control their somatic problem. They may have to work on accepting it, learning to tolerate the discomfort as best as they can (using mindfulness), and carrying on with life as best as possible. Talk to clients about the value of persevering through adversity.

- Clients can also benefit from identifying a valued life activity that they can commit to as a way of countering their somatic discomfort and obsessive focus. For example, a child may decide to learn to play guitar or become an Eagle Scout and commit to all that is required to accomplish this goal, as opposed to dwelling on the somatic problem.

- Kids with somatic concerns are often not in touch with their emotions or thoughts other than those associated with their somatic distress. As a result, they often have an underlying anxiety issue that needs to be identified and dealt with. Mood monitoring (Chapter 5) and cognitive processing (Chapter 7) can help them identify their emotions and thoughts, as well as the situational triggers for their anxiety (other than those associated with their somatic distress). Once these triggers, thoughts, and feelings are identified, you can use other CBT interventions (e.g., behavioral activation, cognitive restructuring, social skills training, etc.) to help manage these issues. However, this is a delicate process that is best addressed after you have taught your clients the other skills previously described here.

- Finally, use exposure therapy techniques to help them persevere through their somatic discomfort and maintain involvement in various potentially rewarding activities. Develop a somatic discomfort hierarchy that rank orders their somatic complaints, and have them select a mild to moderate somatic concern they are willing work on. Then, identify some cognitive and behavioral coping skills (e.g., rational appraisal of their somatic problem, mindful deep breathing, distraction, acceptance) that they can use to tolerate staying involved in an important activity despite their somatic discomfort. Use imaginal exposure to help them practice their coping plan with you first, and then implement in-vivo exposure to help them stay involved in an important real-life activity even in the face of somatic discomfort.

- It is also helpful to talk to clients about excessive "safety behaviors." Kids who are somatically oriented are generally hypersensitive to physical cues, which triggers a variety of behaviors that they think or hope will alleviate their discomfort. These safety behaviors are generally not productive and reinforce an obsessive focus on finding a cure for the condition, which is unlikely. Help clients realistically assess how much benefit they have actually obtained, or are likely to obtain, from their safety behaviors. Help them do a pros and cons analysis of engaging in safety behaviors versus working on accepting their discomfort and persevering.

- Working with somatic symptom disorder is challenging because clients are typically extremely wedded to the idea that their symptoms have a physical cause and cure, and they are skeptical of any explanations or interventions that are psychological in nature. In addition, kids with this condition often lack psychological mindedness and compensate for this through their somatic focus. That is, all problems are reduced to their somatic issues. It is quite a challenge to help them develop a psychological orientation to their somatic problems and their life in general. Progress is generally slow, and you will need to continually validate their somatic distress while simultaneously encouraging psychological mindedness and the use of various CBT interventions to persevere through somatic distress and maintain involvement in healthy and potentially rewarding activities.

CHAPTER TWELVE

Managing Self-Harm and Suicidal Urges:
Evidence-Based Practices to Prevent Suicide and Self-Harm

According to the Centers for Disease Control, suicide was the second leading cause of death among young people 14 to 24 years of age (Heron, 2018). More young people died from suicide than from cancer, heart disease, birth defects, influenza, and pneumonia combined. In addition, the death rate for suicide among youth ages 10–19 increased 56% between 2007 and 2016 (Curtin, Heron, Miniño, & Warner, 2018). Clearly, suicide is a serious matter among young people in this country, and we know that depression, anxiety, and other mental health conditions increase the risk for suicide. Therefore, any mental health professional working with children and adolescents should expect to encounter a potentially suicidal youth.

Fortunately, mental health professionals and epidemiologists have been studying youth suicide and have provided us with some excellent information and clinical tools to help prevent its occurrence (Brent et al., 2011). For example, we know a lot about the risk factors and warning signs of youth suicide (CDC, 2018). In terms of risk factors, we know that males are much more likely to complete suicide, while females are much more likely to attempt suicide. We also know that having a mental disorder increases risk, as does knowing someone who has completed suicide, having a chronic illness, LGBTQ status, prior trauma or abuse, relationship loss, and a prior suicide attempt (especially in the past three to six months). Similarly, we know that warning signs of imminent suicide risk include making specific suicide plans, communicating about suicide or death, or visiting others to "say goodbye."

While an astute clinician is aware of these risk factors and warning signs, this awareness is not sufficient. Rather, a good clinician must also have knowledge regarding prevention strategies, including how to conduct an evidence-based safety plan, how to promote a desire to live even in the face of life's struggles, and how to build skills necessary to resolve a crisis and promote mental functioning over time. In addition, clinicians working with children and adolescents must be adept at communicating and intervening not only with minor clients, but also with their parents or guardians, in the event of a crisis.

This chapter will help you assess youth suicide risk and warning signs, and it will also teach you how to conduct a state-of-the-art, evidence-based suicide prevention safety plan. In addition, evidence-based skills designed to prevent self-harm and suicide are presented. You can use these materials to help high-risk kids identify reasons for living, deconstruct a self-harm or suicide crisis, utilize self-soothing skills, practice acceptance to tolerate difficult situations, and develop a coping plan to manage self-harm and suicide triggers. Although methods to engage the parents or guardians of minors are briefly addressed here, this topic is more thoroughly discussed in the context of parental involvement in Chapter 13.

Risk Factors for Youth Suicide

- Assess your client's suicide risk factors based on your evaluation and knowledge of that child or adolescent.

- Check off any risk factors that your client has.

- There is no scientifically developed cutoff score to identify suicide risk. However, the risk of suicide is greater the more risk factors that your client has.

- Discuss these risk factors with your client and develop a suicide prevention safety plan if indicated.

Risk Factors for Youth Suicide

· ·

Check off any of the following risk factors for suicide that your client exhibits:

☐ Previous suicide attempt (Note: Risk of re-attempt is greatest three to six months post-suicide attempt)

☐ Mental illness (e.g., depression, bipolar disorder, schizophrenia, borderline personality disorder, PTSD)

☐ Male (Note: Although women are more likely to attempt suicide, men are four times as likely to complete suicide)

☐ Substance abuse and/or alcohol disorders

☐ History of abuse or mistreatment

☐ Family problems (e.g., family history of suicide, parental mental health problems, parent-child conflict)

☐ Serious or chronic physical illness

☐ Feelings of hopelessness

☐ Psychological traits (e.g., impulsivity, emotional dysregulation, poor problem-solving skills, aggressive tendencies)

☐ Prolonged stress (e.g., harassment, bullying, relationship problems)

☐ Relationship loss

☐ Isolation (e.g., lack of social support; excessive social media, video game, and Internet involvement)

☐ Easy access to lethal methods (e.g., firearms) for completing suicide

☐ Exposure to others who have committed suicide

☐ LGBTQ

Youth Suicide Protective Factors

- Identify the protective factors your client has based on your evaluation and knowledge of that child or adolescent.

- Protective factors can include the client's own personal characteristics and/or environmental circumstances.

- Given that protective factors can help mitigate your client's suicide risk, discuss how you and your client can work to strengthen these protective factors. Help kids become more aware of their strengths and take pro-active action to consciously use these strengths in their daily lives. For example, if a youth has athletic talent, help them understand how special this talent is and help them focus on using this strength to their best ability. Help them notice how their mastery of athletics impacts their mood and the lives of others.

- Discuss ways in which to reduce your client's access to available methods for suicide and take practical action to reduce or remove any lethal means.

Youth Suicide Protective Factors

· ·

Check off any of the following protective factors for suicide that your client exhibits:

☐ Effective clinical care for mental, physical, and substance abuse disorders

☐ Easy access to a variety of clinical interventions and support for help seeking

☐ Connectedness to family, friends, community, and social institutions

☐ Support from ongoing medical and mental health care relationships

☐ Skills in problem solving, conflict resolution, and nonviolent ways of handling disputes

☐ Cultural and religious beliefs that discourage suicide and support instincts for self-preservation

☐ Restricted access to lethal means

Youth Suicide Warning Signs

- Identifying suicide warning signs in your clients is important in mitigating imminent suicide risk.

- Inquire whether clients have talked about killing themselves, feeling hopeless, having no reason to live, being a burden to others, feeling trapped, or experiencing unbearable pain.

- In addition, look to see if clients have exhibited one or more of the following behaviors: increased use of alcohol or drugs, looking for a way to end their lives (e.g., searching online for methods), withdrawing from activities, isolating from family and friends, sleeping too much or too little, visiting or calling people to say goodbye, giving away prized possessions, or exhibiting an increase in aggression or fatigue.

- Finally, look for a change in any of the following: depression, anxiety, loss of interest, irritability, humiliation/shame, agitation/anger, or relief/sudden improvement.

- There is no specific cutoff score to indicate how serious or imminent the risk is. However, a greater number of warning signs, as well as those that have occurred more recently, is indicative of increased risk.

- Use the following checklist to discuss warning signs with your clients and their parents.

- Involve parents when there is an imminent risk of suicide as indicated by the presence of significant warning signs.

Youth Suicide Warning Signs Checklist

· · · · · · · · · · · · · · · · · · ·

Have you been thinking, doing, or feeling like any of the following? Check all that apply, including in the past week and the past three months.

	Past Week	Past 3 Months
Communicated with anyone about suicidal thoughts or intentions?		
Felt hopeless?		
Felt like there was no reason to live?		
Felt like a burden to others?		
Felt trapped?		
Felt as if you were in unbearable pain?		
Experienced depressed mood?		
Increased use of alcohol or drugs?		
Looked for a way to end your life?		
Isolated yourself from family and friends?		
Been sleeping too much or too little?		
Visited or called people to say goodbye?		
Given away prized possessions?		
Been more agitated or aggressive?		
Been more fatigued?		
Been more anxious?		
Lost interest in doing things that you enjoy?		
Been more irritable?		
Felt humiliated or ashamed?		
Felt relieved or as if things were suddenly better?		

Conduct an Evidence-Based Suicide Risk Assessment

- The Columbia-Suicide Severity Rating Scale (C-SSRS) is a state-of-the-art, evidence-based suicide risk assessment instrument (Posner et al., 2011).

- It is routinely used in assessing suicide risk and has been shown in research to be an effective tool in assessing suicide risk and preventing suicide.

- The "Lifetime/Recent" version of the C-SSRS is presented on the following pages for your use. This instrument is appropriate for children ages six and up.

- For younger children (ages four to five), use the "Very Young Child – Cognitively Impaired" version, which is available at the C-SSRS website (http://cssrs.columbia.edu/). Clinicians are encouraged to become trained in using the C-SSRS prior to implementing it.

- Upon sufficient training, you can use the C-SSRS to conduct a suicide risk assessment when the risk factors and warning signs indicate that an assessment is needed.

Worksheet

Columbia-Suicide Severity Rating Scale (C-SSRS)

SUICIDAL IDEATION				
Ask questions 1 and 2. If both are negative, proceed to "Suicidal Behavior" section. If the answer to question 2 is "yes", ask questions 3, 4 and 5. If the answer to question 1 and/or 2 is "yes", complete "Intensity of Ideation" section.	**Lifetime: Time He/She Felt Most Suicidal**		**Past 1 month**	
1. Wish to be Dead Subject endorses thoughts about a wish to be dead or not alive anymore, or wish to fall asleep and not wake up. Have you wished you were dead or wished you could go to sleep and not wake up? If yes, describe:	Yes ☐	No ☐	Yes ☐	No ☐
2. Non-Specific Active Suicidal Thoughts General non-specific thoughts of wanting to end one's life/commit suicide (e.g., "I've thought about killing myself ") without thoughts of ways to kill oneself/associated methods, intent, or plan during the assessment period. Have you actually had any thoughts of killing yourself? If yes, describe:	Yes ☐	No ☐	Yes ☐	No ☐
3. Active Suicidal Ideation with Any Methods (Not Plan) without Intent to Act Subject endorses thoughts of suicide and has thought of at least one method during the assessment period. This is different than a specific plan with time, place or method details worked out (e.g., thought of method to kill self but not a specific plan). Includes person who would say, *"I thought about taking an overdose but I never made a specific plan as to when, where or how I would actually do it . . . and I would never go through with it."* ***Have you been thinking about how you might do this?*** If yes, describe:	Yes ☐	No ☐	Yes ☐	No ☐
4. Active Suicidal Ideation with Some Intent to Act, without Specific Plan Active suicidal thoughts of killing oneself and subject reports having some intent to act on such thoughts, as opposed to *"I have the thoughts but I definitely will not do anything about them."* ***Have you had these thoughts and had some intention of acting on them?*** If yes, describe:	Yes ☐	No ☐	Yes ☐	No ☐

	Lifetime: Time He/She Felt Most Suicidal		Past 1 month	

5. Active Suicidal Ideation with Specific Plan and Intent

Thoughts of killing oneself with details of plan fully or partially worked out and subject has some intent to carry it out.

Have you started to work out or worked out the details of how to kill yourself? Do you intend to carry out this plan?

If yes, describe:

	Yes ☐	No ☐	Yes ☐	No ☐

INTENSITY OF IDEATION

The following features should be rated with respect to the most severe type of ideation (e.g., 1-5 from prior section, with 1 being the least severe and 5 being the most severe). Ask about time he/she was feeling the most suicidal.

<u>Lifetime</u> **- Most Severe Ideation:** _____   _____

                         Type # (1-5) Description of Ideation

<u>Recent</u> **- Most Severe Ideation:** _____   _____

                         Type # (1-5) Description of Ideation

Frequency

How many times have you had these thoughts?

(1) Less than once a week   (2) Once a week   (3) 2-5 times in week
(4) Daily or almost daily   (5) Many times each day

_____	_____

Duration

When you have the thoughts how long do they last?

(1) Fleeting - few seconds or minutes
(2) Less than 1 hour/some of the time
(3) 1-4 hours/a lot of time
(4) 4-8 hours/most of day
(5) More than 8 hours/persistent or continuous

_____	_____

Controllability

Could/can you stop thinking about killing yourself or wanting to die if you want to?

(1) Easily able to control thoughts
(2) Can control thoughts with little difficulty
(3) Can control thoughts with some difficulty
(4) Can control thoughts with a lot of difficulty
(5) Unable to control thoughts
(0) Does not attempt to control thoughts

_____	_____

<table>
<tr><td colspan="3">

Deterrents

Are there things - anyone or anything (e.g., family, religion, pain of death) - that stopped you from wanting to die or acting on thoughts of committing suicide?

(1) Deterrents definitely stopped you from attempting suicide

(2) Deterrents probably stopped you

(3) Uncertain that deterrents stopped you

(4) Deterrents most likely did not stop you

(5) Deterrents definitely did not stop you

(0) Does not apply

</td></tr>
</table>

Deterrents *Are there things - anyone or anything (e.g., family, religion, pain of death) - that stopped you from wanting to die or acting on thoughts of committing suicide?* (1) Deterrents definitely stopped you from attempting suicide (2) Deterrents probably stopped you (3) Uncertain that deterrents stopped you (4) Deterrents most likely did not stop you (5) Deterrents definitely did not stop you (0) Does not apply	⎯⎯	⎯⎯
Reasons for Ideation *What sort of reasons did you have for thinking about wanting to die or killing yourself? Was it to end the pain or stop the way you were feeling (in other words you couldn't go on living with this pain or how you were feeling) or was it to get attention, revenge or a reaction from others? Or both?* (1) Completely to get attention, revenge or a reaction from others (2) Mostly to get attention, revenge or a reaction from others (3) Equally to get attention, revenge or a reaction from others and to end/stop the pain (4) Mostly to end or stop the pain (you couldn't go on living with the pain or how you were feeling) (5) Completely to end or stop the pain (you couldn't go on living with the pain or how you were feeling) (0) Does not apply	⎯⎯	⎯⎯

SUICIDAL BEHAVIOR *(Check all that apply, so long as these are separate events; must ask about all types)*	**Lifetime**		**Past 3 months**	
Actual Attempt: A potentially self-injurious act committed with at least some wish to die, *as a result of act*. Behavior was in part thought of as method to kill oneself. Intent does not have to be 100%. If there is **any** intent/desire to die associated with the act, then it can be considered an actual suicide attempt. *There does not have to be any injury or harm*, just the potential for injury or harm. If person pulls trigger while gun is in mouth but gun is broken so no injury results, this is considered an attempt. Inferring Intent: Even if an individual denies intent/wish to die, it may be inferred clinically from the behavior or circumstances. For example, a highly lethal act that is clearly not an accident so no other intent but suicide can be inferred (e.g., gunshot to head, jumping from window of a high floor/story). Also, if someone denies intent to die, but they thought that what they did could be lethal, intent may be inferred. *Have you made a suicide attempt?* *Have you done anything to harm yourself?* *Have you done anything dangerous where you could have died?*	Yes ☐	No ☐	Yes ☐	No ☐
	Total # of attempts ⎯⎯		Total # of attempts ⎯⎯	

	Yes	No	Yes	No
What did you do? *Did you_____ as a way to end your life?* *Did you want to die (even a little) when you____?* *Were you trying to end your life when you ____?* *Or Did you think it was possible you could have died from____?* *Or did you do it purely for other reasons / without ANY intention of killing yourself (like to relieve stress, feel better, get sympathy, or get something else to happen)?* (Self-Injurious Behavior without suicidal intent) If yes, describe: **Has subject engaged in Non-Suicidal Self-Injurious Behavior?**	**Yes** ☐	**No** ☐	**Yes** ☐	**No** ☐
Interrupted Attempt: When the person is interrupted (by an outside circumstance) from starting the potentially self-injurious act *(if not for that, actual attempt would have occurred).* Overdose: Person has pills in hand but is stopped from ingesting. Once they ingest any pills, this becomes an attempt rather than an interrupted attempt. Shooting: Person has gun pointed toward self, gun is taken away by someone else, or is somehow prevented from pulling trigger. Once they pull the trigger, even if the gun fails to fire, it is an attempt. Jumping: Person is poised to jump, is grabbed and taken down from ledge. Hanging: Person has noose around neck but has not yet started to hang - is stopped from doing so. *Has there been a time when you started to do something to end your life but someone or something stopped you before you actually did anything?* If yes, describe:	**Yes** ☐ Total # of interrupted ____	**No** ☐	**Yes** ☐ Total # of interrupted ____	**No** ☐
Aborted or Self-Interrupted Attempt: When person begins to take steps toward making a suicide attempt, but stops themselves before they actually have engaged in any self-destructive behavior. Examples are similar to interrupted attempts, except that the individual stops him/herself, instead of being stopped by something else. *Has there been a time when you started to do something to try to end your life but you stopped yourself before you actually did anything?* If yes, describe:	**Yes** ☐ Total # of aborted or self-interrupted ____	**No** ☐	**Yes** ☐ Total # of aborted or self-interrupted ____	**No** ☐
Preparatory Acts or Behavior: Acts or preparation towards imminently making a suicide attempt. This can include anything beyond a verbalization or thought, such as assembling a specific method (e.g., buying pills, purchasing a gun) or preparing for one's death by suicide (e.g., giving things away, writing a suicide note). *Have you taken any steps towards making a suicide attempt or preparing to kill yourself (such as collecting pills, getting a gun, giving valuables away or writing a suicide note)?* If yes, describe:	**Yes** ☐ Total # of preparatory acts ____	**No** ☐	**Yes** ☐ Total # of preparatory acts ____	**No** ☐

	Most Recent Attempt Date:	Most Lethal Attempt Date:	Initial/First Attempt Date:
Actual Lethality/Medical Damage: 0. No physical damage or very minor physical damage (e.g., surface scratches). 1. Minor physical damage (e.g., lethargic speech; first-degree burns; mild bleeding; sprains). 2. Moderate physical damage; medical attention needed (e.g., conscious but sleepy, somewhat responsive; second-degree burns; bleeding of major vessel). 3. Moderately severe physical damage; *medical* hospitalization and likely intensive care required (e.g., comatose with reflexes intact; third-degree burns less than 20% of body; extensive blood loss but can recover; major fractures). 4. Severe physical damage; *medical* hospitalization with intensive care required (e.g., comatose without reflexes; third-degree burns over 20% of body; extensive blood loss with unstable vital signs; major damage to a vital area). 5. Death	*Enter Code* _____	*Enter Code* _____	*Enter Code* _____
Potential Lethality: Only Answer if Actual Lethality=0 Likely lethality of actual attempt if no medical damage (the following examples, while having no actual medical damage, had potential for very serious lethality: put gun in mouth and pulled the trigger but gun fails to fire so no medical damage; laying on train tracks with oncoming train but pulled away before run over). 0 = Behavior not likely to result in injury 1 = Behavior likely to result in injury but not likely to cause death 2 = Behavior likely to result in death despite available medical care	*Enter Code* _____	*Enter Code* _____	*Enter Code* _____

Reprinted with permission for *CBT Toolbox for Depressed, Anxious and Suicidal Children and Adolescents.*

Develop an Evidence-Based Suicide Prevention Safety Plan

- Conduct a suicide safety plan if your clients acknowledge any of the following in the past three months:

    o Wanting to be dead

    o Has contemplated a suicide plan or method

    o Has attempted suicide (e.g., any self-harm behavior where the client's stated intent was to die *even if* the self-harm behavior was unlikely to cause death by your estimation)

- Your clients' verbal or written agreement to not commit suicide (e.g., non-suicide contract) **is not** a valid or ethical suicide prevention safety plan.

- Use an evidence-based suicide prevention safety plan, such as the safety plan on the following page developed by Drs. Barbara Stanley and Gregory Brown (2012). It's recommended that you register at the Suicide Prevention Resource Center website to receive more information about the plan (www. suicidesafetyplan.com) and that you obtain online training in implementing the plan as well (http:// zerosuicide.sprc.org/sites/zerosuicide.sprc.org/files/sp/course.htm).

- To develop the safety plan, first discuss warning signs for suicide with your clients, including trigger situations and their thoughts, feelings, and behaviors associated with the trigger.

- Then, help clients identify some coping skills that they can use on their own without involving anyone else. This is the preferred coping strategy because we want clients to have the skills to manage these urges on their own if possible.

- If they can't quell the urges on their own, the next best strategy is to involve a trusted other but without disclosing their suicide urges.

- If this approach is not helpful, then it is recommended that they contact a trusted other and discuss their suicide urges.

- If discussing their suicide urges with a trusted other does not help the urge subside, then it is appropriate to contact a professional.

- A suicide prevention safety plan should always include a discussion of means reduction. Discuss the methods for suicide that your client has thought about. Identify practical methods to reduce access to these methods.

- Finally, help your client identify some reasons for living, but be sure to communicate empathy for their feelings of hopelessness as well.

- In addition, it's important to involve parents in the development and/or implementation of this safety plan. If the minor client is an imminent suicide risk (as indicated by the C-SSRS and your judgment), then you are obligated to share this information with the parent *even if* the minor client does not agree.

My Safety Plan

. . . .

Step 1: Warning signs (thoughts, images, mood, situation, behavior) that a crisis may be developing:

1. _____

2. _____

3. _____

Step 2: Internal coping strategies – Things I can do to take my mind off my problems without contacting another person (relaxation technique, physical activity):

1. _____

2. _____

3. _____

Step 3: People and social settings that provide distraction:

1. Name: _____ Phone: _____

2. Name: _____ Place: _____

3. Name: _____ Place: _____

Step 4: People whom I can ask for help:

1. Name: _____ Phone: _____

2. Name: _____ Phone: _____

3. Name: _____ Place: _____

Step 5: Professionals or agencies I can contact during a crisis:

1. Clinician Name: _____ Phone: _____

    Clinician Pager or Emergency Contact # _____

2. Clinician Name: _____ Phone: _____

    Clinician Pager or Emergency Contact # _____

3. Local Emergency Department: _____ Phone: _____

    Urgent Care Services Address _____

    Urgent Care Services Phones _____

4. Suicide Prevention Lifeline Phone: 1-800-273-TALK (8255)

Step 6: Making my environment safe:

1. _____

2. _____

The one thing that is most important to me and worth living for is:

_____

Behavioral Chain Analysis

- If your clients have engaged in any self-harm behavior or suicidal behavior in the past three months, conduct a "behavioral chain analysis" (or "chain") to examine all of the factors that led up to the behavior (Linehan, 1993).

- Before beginning, assess your clients' capacity to manage this intervention. Behavioral chain analysis is a powerful intervention and may not be appropriate with clients who are having strong suicide or self-harm urges, are psychotic, or are prone to dissociation.

- Be sure to fully explain the procedure, its risks and benefits, and obtain informed consent.

- Explain that behavioral chain analysis can teach them how to better manage a suicide or self-harm crisis in the future by helping them deconstruct the specific factors that led up to their recent crisis.

- Invite your clients to close their eyes and take some deep, slow breaths.

- Ask them to visualize being in the situation where they had their self-harm or suicide crisis. Ask them to visualize the specific details of the situation, including the various aspects of their environment; their thoughts, feelings, and behaviors; and the behaviors of others. The more detailed the description, the better.

- It is likely that your clients will provide an abbreviated description of the incident at first. Slow down the process and ask them to visualize and describe important details they may have passed over. Be sure not to miss the essential elements of their experience. The point is to make the chain as detailed as possible.

- Praise and support your clients' courage for disclosing these details throughout the process.

- Pause and check your clients' SUDS ratings throughout the process as indicated.

- Discontinue the behavioral chain analysis if clients are unable to manage the distress of recounting the experience, and help them become re-grounded and safe.

- Therapists are encouraged to visit the Dialectical Behavior Therapy website for further information and training in Behavioral Chain Analysis. (https://behavioraltech.org)

Behavioral Chain Analysis

It is helpful to examine what happened after a tough experience. Behavioral chain analysis helps you break down a complex and sometimes stressful experience by going through the specific details that led up to the situation. First, you identify what made you more vulnerable to hurting yourself. Then, you identify the triggering event – that is, what started you on this chain of events. You look into detail about what you were feeling, thinking, and doing at the time, as well as what was going on around you. When you do a behavioral chain, you can see the specific steps that led to your problem behavior and the consequences of that behavior.

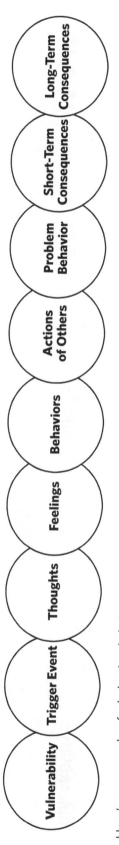

| Vulnerability | Trigger Event | Thoughts | Feelings | Behaviors | Actions of Others | Problem Behavior | Short-Term Consequences | Long-Term Consequences |

Here's an example of a behavioral chain:

Vulnerability	Trigger Event	Thoughts	Feelings	Behaviors	Actions of Others	Problem Behavior	Short-Term Consequences	Long-Term Consequences
Not enough sleep; Felt emotionally drained	Suzie didn't sit next to me at lunch today	No one likes me, I'm worthless	Lonely; Sad	I cried and hid in the bathroom	No one else would sit with me	Went home after school and cut myself	Relief; Had to go to hospital to get stitches	Feel even more guilty and sad; Parents loose trust in me

Doing a behavioral chain analysis is helpful because it lets you think of what you could do differently if you had the chance to do it all over again. You can see what link in the "chain" you could change in order to prevent the problem behavior from happening in the future. Remember, changing just one link will change the entire chain – you could have a totally different outcome! So, let's get your behavioral chain started!

Adapted from *Cognitive-behavioral Treatment of Borderline Personality Disorder*, 1993, Marsha Linehan

My Behavioral Chain

Use this guide to help you examine the chain of events that led up to your most recent self-harm behavior or suicide attempt. Identify all of the links in the chain that contributed to this crisis and prompted you to engage in the problem behavior.

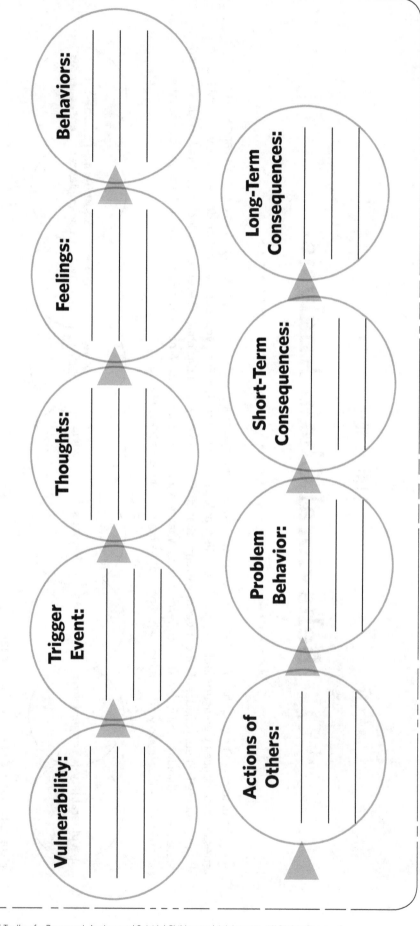

Problem Solve My Chain

- Once clients complete their chain, remind them that they can better manage future suicide or self-harm crises by analyzing the micro-events of their recent crisis.

- Help them problem solve the links in their own chain and identify at least one link that could have been managed better and that may have even prevented the self-harm or suicidal behavior from occurring.

- The link where they could have intervened might include a thought they had, something they did (or didn't do), an action someone else took (or didn't take), something about the circumstances surrounding the crisis, or their understanding of the consequences.

Problem Solve My Chain

· ·

Now that we've identified your chain, let's problem solve. In the first column, use your answers from the "My Behavioral Chain" worksheet to write down the actual chain of events that happened. Then, in the second column, use your problem-solving skills to see if you could change any of the links in the chain. How could you reduce your vulnerability in the future? Are there ways you could prevent the trigger event? How could you think or act differently? Is there anything that someone else could do differently that might help? What would be the consequences of engaging in new, skillful behavior instead of hurting yourself?

Links	Actual Chain of Events	Problem-Solve Solutions
Vulnerability		
Trigger event		
Thoughts		
Feelings		
Behaviors		
Actions of Others		
Problem Behavior		
Short-term Consequences		
Long-term Consequences		

Therapist Tips

Reasons for Self-Harm Behavior

- It's important to validate your client's reasons for self-harm behavior (including that which leads to or culminates in suicide attempts) before discussing reasons for living. Validating their reasons for self-harm will help them feel understood and more open to discussing reasons for living.

- Do not try to alter or challenge their perspective at this point. Simply take the time to validate and understand.

- After clients complete the worksheet, make sure that they are well-grounded and are not experiencing renewed urges to self-harm as a result of doing this exercise.

- If indicated, engage in crisis management to manage any renewed urges.

- Remember, CBT is a process of "guided discovery." Your genuine interest in understanding your clients and their reasons for self-harm behaviors is a powerful way of communicating your non-judgmental commitment to their self-discovery.

Reasons for Self-Harm Behavior

· ·

All behavior has a purpose, and when teens engage in self-harm behavior, they generally do so for a reason. For example, they might self-harm to manage or escape negative feelings, to confirm their negative self-beliefs, or to communicate to others how they are feeling. Check any of the following reasons that you engage in self-harm.

I self-harm ...

☐ So I don't have to think about real problems.

☐ To feel better in the short run.

☐ To reduce or get rid of emotional pain.

☐ To punish myself.

☐ To distract myself from emotional pain.

☐ Because I don't know what else to do.

☐ To show others how much emotional pain I am in.

☐ To boost my self-esteem.

☐ To end my life.

☐ Because other kids say it helps.

☐ To feel in control.

☐ To have a specific someone show some concern for me.

☐ Other (specify): _____

Consequences of Self-Harm Behavior

- Young clients often experience inadvertent positive reinforcement after engaging in self-harm behavior (e.g., a parent may back away from setting needed limits) or fantasize about a positive outcome as a result of their self-harm behavior (e.g., that a romantic partner will return after a break-up).

- In order to draw attention away from these perceived positive effects of self-harm, it's important to help clients identify the realistic consequences of their self-harm behavior.

- Young people have limited insight and judgment regarding the consequences of their actions, especially when applied to the highly emotionally-charged issue of suicide. This worksheet will help them consider the realistic consequences of their self-harm behavior.

- Young clients in this situation are very vulnerable to feeling guilty and judged. Always lead this discussion with respect and empathy, and be careful to avoid any connotation of blame or judgment.

- This discussion is best conducted after they have settled down a bit from the suicide crisis. For example, I have typically conducted this discussion with clients one to three weeks after they have been admitted to a psychiatric hospital for a suicide attempt, or on an outpatient basis following discharge from a psychiatric hospitalization due to a suicide attempt.

- Using the following checklist can help facilitate this discussion by providing a structure that will help young clients organize and disclose their conflicted thoughts and feelings on this issue.

Consequences of Self-Harm Behavior

. . . .

Self-harm behavior may provide some relief in the short run, but it has long-term consequences that are more serious. Put a checkmark by any consequences that you have experienced, or could experience, as a result of engaging in self-harm behavior.

☐ I have scars on my body.

☐ I have to go to counseling.

☐ I have been admitted to a psychiatric hospital.

☐ I'm in physical pain afterwards.

☐ My parents don't trust me.

☐ I need to seek out emergency medical treatment.

☐ I still feel stressed afterwards.

☐ It doesn't really solve my problems.

☐ I get a bad reputation with my peers.

☐ I become too dependent upon self-harm behavior to cope.

☐ My parents, family members, and friends are upset with me.

☐ Other (specify): _____

Positive Consequences of Resisting Self-Harm Behaviors

- Young clients may need help identifying the positive outcomes of resisting their self-harm urges.

- It can be difficult for young people to identify these on their own because the depression and intense emotional arousal they experience during a crisis prevents them from realistically appraising how their life could get better if they were to persevere through the crisis and fight the self-harm urges.

- Use the following checklist to help clients think of the positive consequences of resisting self-harm urges. Some of these may be more short-term benefits (e.g., they don't have to be hospitalized), whereas others involve more long-term benefits (e.g., improved trust with parents). Be sure to emphasize both, as this can help motivate them to persevere through these urges.

- Similar to when it is advisable to have a discussion of negative consequences, this discussion is also best conducted after clients have settled down a bit from the suicide crisis.

Positive Consequences of Resisting Self-Harm Behaviors

· ·

Let's take some time to think about how your life might be better if you can resist the urge to engage in self-harm behavior. In what ways might your life get better?

☐ I won't be hospitalized.

☐ I will have a healthy body.

☐ I won't be in as much physical pain.

☐ My parents will trust me.

☐ I can get more freedom and privileges.

☐ I will feel better about myself.

☐ I will learn to solve problems in a healthy manner.

☐ I can have more fun.

☐ I will be able to reach my life goals.

☐ I will have more friends.

☐ I can live life to the fullest.

☐ I will have a better reputation with my peers.

☐ My parents, family, and friends won't always be upset with me.

☐ Other (specify): _____

Pros and Cons of Self-Harm Behavior or Ending My Life

- While a challenge, it can be quite therapeutic to have an open discussion of the pros and cons of self-harm and suicide.

- Acknowledging that there are both pros and cons to this problem behavior can be validating for clients who likely have strong ambivalence regarding their self-harm urges. It helps them consider reasons to resist hurting themselves without feeling invalidated.

- When completing the exercise, be sure to remain unbiased and to not challenge their perspective. Rather, focus on understanding their perspective and validating it. This is particularly important when asking clients to consider the cons of self-harm or suicide.

- It can be helpful to ask clients open-ended questions about the negative consequences of self-harm or suicide, or to gently prompt them if they are struggling to identify the cons themselves.

Pros and Cons of Self-Harm Behavior or Ending My Life

· ·

Use this worksheet to identify some of the pros of engaging in self-harm behavior or attempting suicide, as well as some of its cons.

	Pros	Cons
Engaging in Self-Harm Behavior or Ending My Life		
Resisting Self-Harm Behavior and Suicidal Urges		

Therapist Tips

Reasons for Living

- Once you have validated clients' reasons for self-harm, you are more likely to have a productive discussion regarding their reasons for living.

- Ask clients to discuss their personal strengths and the positives in their life.

- Young clients who are depressed and suicidal will need some prompting with this discussion. Remind them that we all have some strengths, but remember to maintain a Socratic posture; young clients with depression are very good at dismissing compliments. For example, ask strategic questions that you are pretty sure you know the answer to, like: "Weren't you on the Honor Roll last marking period? Would that be a strength?"

- Ask Socratic questions with a genuine degree of curiosity, such as: "Ok, you don't believe that your parents care about you. Can you tell me more about this and help me understand?" This is a chance to learn a lot about your clients if you are truly listening and trying to understand.

- Identifying strengths will likely be a challenge for your clients. However, if you've validated their struggles, then they will be more open to your prompting them about their strengths.

Reasons for Living

· ·

When you are really stressed, it can be hard to think of reasons for living. Answer the following questions and make a list of reasons for living. Whenever you are having an urge to hurt yourself, you can look back at the list to help you keep a positive outlook on life.

1. What are the positives in your life? _____

   _____

   _____

2. What are your talents and strengths? _____

   _____

   _____

3. Who cares about you? _____

   _____

   _____

4. What do you think the consequences will be for you if you engage in self-harm behavior or complete suicide? _____

   _____

   _____

5. What impact do you think it would have on other people in your life? _____

   _____

   _____

6. What are the things you want to do in your life that you haven't done yet? What are your future goals? _____

_____

_____

7. Now, think about your answers and make a list of some reasons for living. _____

_____

_____

_____

_____

_____

My Hope Box

- We all have a set of treasured personal items that represent positive memories for us. These items might include photos, personal artifacts, or memorabilia that depict a special time or experience in our life. These items help us recall the special times in our lives and provide us with meaning and hope.

- Invite your clients to identify the personal artifacts that they hold dear and that represent meaning and hope for them.

- Ask them to collect these items and place them in an old shoe box, which they can decorate. This will become their "Hope Box."

- Clients can periodically look at the items in their Hope Box, especially when they are distressed and in need of some hope and encouragement to get them through the difficult moment.

- When looking through their Hope Box, encourage your clients to ponder the special meaning of the items and how their life has meaning.

Worksheet

My Hope Box

. . . .

It helps to focus on something that has special meaning for you when you are feeling depressed or having the urge to hurt yourself. For example, it can be very soothing to look over some personal items that you hold dear, like special photos, meaningful letters, inspirational writings, a favorite CD, a special card, a religious article, or some special knick-knack. Looking through these items can give you hope and courage.

Make a collection of some meaningful items that have special value to you. Then, collect the items, place them in an old shoe box, and decorate the box to make it look special. We'll call this your "Hope Box." Whenever you are feeling stressed out, you can go through your Hope Box and think of the special meaning that each item in the box has for you. These items can give you some hope and get you through a rough time.

What are some special items you can put in your Hope Box?

1. _____

2. _____

3. _____

4. _____

5. _____

Emotional Distress Tolerance

- Remind clients of the "amygdala hijack" and the importance of calming the "emotional brain" when they are distressed so that they can access their "rational thinking, problem-solving brain."

- Encourage them to identify some mindfulness skills that they can use when experiencing self-harm urges.

- Help them understand that the urge to self-harm will eventually subside if they can just find a way to soothe themselves.

- Encourage them to do a behavioral experiment with self-soothing activities that involve the different senses (sight, sound, smell, taste, and touch).

- Help them practice distress tolerance skills in your office so they can use them in real-life situations when needed.

Worksheet

Emotional Distress Tolerance

· ·

When you are feeling the urge to hurt yourself, you can help reduce your stress level by engaging your five senses: sight, sound, smell, taste, and touch. Activities that engage these senses will naturally help you to relax and get past the urge. Make a list of different sensory activities that you could do to help you get through a difficult situation. Remember: It's important to practice these activities on a regular basis so you can more easily use them whenever you are in a crisis.

Sight	What things could you look at, or picture in your mind, to help you relax? (e.g., pictures of happy memories, funny comics)
Sound	What are some relaxing sounds you could listen to? (e.g., a favorite music playlist, nature sounds)
Smell	What are some pleasing scents that you could smell? (e.g., aromatherapy oils, freshly baked cookies)
Taste	What types of flavors could you eat that are enjoyable? (e.g., chocolate, sour candies)
Touch	What types of things could you touch that you find soothing? (e.g., playdough, hand lotion)

Future Time Imaging

- Young clients can improve their chances of reaching their goals by imagining themselves doing the tasks that will get them to their goals and by visualizing themselves actually achieving them. This technique is often used by athletes prior to an athletic performance. When athletes visualize themselves performing well in their upcoming competition, it improves their actual performance.

- Invite your clients to close their eyes and do some deep breathing.

- Prompt them to imagine themselves doing what they need to do to reach their future goals. Maybe it's studying for and passing a test. Or, perhaps it's tolerating a disappointment and moving forward in life with confidence and optimism.

- Invite them to imagine themselves achieving their future goals, including what it would feel like, what they would be thinking, and what they and others would be doing.

- Encourage them to visualize the positive experience of achieving their future goals.

Worksheet

Future Time Imaging

· ·

When you are feeling the urge to hurt yourself, it can be helpful to imagine yourself doing well and reaching your goals in the future. Even if you aren't sure that you can reach your goals, it is still helpful to imagine yourself achieving them in the future. Visualizing yourself doing well in the future can help make it come true! This technique is called future time imaging, and it is a trick that athletes often use to get ready before a big game. When they imagine themselves performing well in the upcoming game, it actually helps enhance their performance! Let's start by describing what you would like to be doing in the future.

Describe what you would like to be doing **six months** from now.
Describe what you would like to be doing **one year** from now.
Describe what you would you like to be doing in **five years**.

Now, close your eyes and imagine yourself achieving these goals. Imagine all the details you possibly can, especially what you are doing and how you are feeling. Don't let any negative images come into your mind. Keep imagining everything positive that you will be doing in the future as you reach your goals. Let yourself imagine how happy and proud you would be.

Using Acceptance to Tolerate Difficult Situations

- Most of us will encounter something in our life that is beyond our ability to change. When this happens, it's often better to accept the reality of the situation, instead of trying to change it and becoming frustrated when we are unable to. However, acceptance is easier said than done.

- One way to help people accept difficult realities is to have them put positive energy into some activity that they value deeply. For example, "Mothers Against Drunk Drivers" was founded by a mother who lost her daughter to a drunk driving accident. This organization has made a big difference on how we as a society deal with drunk drivers. In addition, their advocacy has helped many parents accept the tragic loss of their child.

- This is what we want to help our clients understand and do: commit themselves to a valued, altruistic activity that will bring a sense of pride and purpose.

- Discuss the concept of acceptance with your clients using the following handout.

- Then, help them identify something that is frustrating them but that is beyond their ability to change. Perhaps their parents are getting divorced and there is nothing they can do about this. Or, perhaps they have a medical condition that they have to endure even with the best medical care. Or, perhaps they have experienced a relationship loss.

- Help clients identify a valued, altruistic activity that they can commit to doing that will help them accept this difficult reality. Encourage them to persevere with this committed action.

Handout

What is Acceptance?

. . . .

Most of us will encounter something in our life that is beyond our ability to change. Maybe a kid's parents are getting a divorce and there is nothing the kid can do to change their minds. Or, maybe a kid gets diagnosed with diabetes and has to manage this condition the rest of his or her life. When this happens, it's often better to accept the reality of the situation, as opposed to trying to change it and becoming frustrated when we are unable to. Acceptance doesn't mean that we approve of what has happened to us. It just means that we understand that we can't change it, and we are willing to move on.

It's really hard to accept something that really upsets us. Naturally, we want to change it, and people generally do everything they can to try to change something they really don't like. They might think, "It shouldn't have to be this way." And they're right! But there is a difference between the way it "should be" and the way "it is." You've heard the saying, "It is what it is," right? Well, that's what acceptance is. You can't change the final score of the championship basketball game you lost because "it is what it is." But you could accept the loss and commit to working as hard as you can in the off season to get better for next year.

One way to accept difficult situations is to focus your attention on something that is really important to you and that other people would consider a really positive thing to do. Something that is really important to you is called a "value." In other words, you can accept difficult situations by turning your attention to something you "value." For example, if a kid is diagnosed with diabetes, he or she might volunteer to help raise money for diabetes research. But reaching this positive goal will not be easy, and the kid will have to make a commitment to work hard to reach this goal. That means that in order to reach real acceptance, you have to identify a valued activity and then make a commitment to making it happen.

This is what we will work on in this session: identifying what you need to accept, as well as what you value and choose to commit to.

Using Acceptance to Tolerate Difficult Situations

· ·

Is there something in your life that is beyond your control to change, even if you worked your hardest to make it better? Think about whether it might be better to accept this issue for what it is (rather than fighting it) and write it in the "What I Need to Accept" column.

Then, think of something important that you could do to make your life, or someone else's life, more positive. Something that is really important to you and that would be really beneficial for you or someone else. Make a specific plan on how you will follow up on your commitment, and write this in the "What I Value and Will Commit To" column.

Use your mindfulness meditation skills to "visualize" yourself accepting this difficult matter. Let your troubling thoughts about this issue come into your mind, and then let these thoughts go like a leaf floating down a river. Once you have let the troubling thoughts go, visualize yourself committing to your valued action and feeling better.

What I Need to Accept	What I Value and Will Commit To

Therapist Tips

Problem Solving in a Crisis

- Advise clients that they will very likely need to use good problem-solving skills to manage a self-harm or suicide crisis.

- Review the problem-solving steps and ground rules discussed in Chapter 9.

- Use problem solving to identify a positive way to manage the self-harm or suicide urge.

- Remember the ground rule: There is no such thing as a bad option when brainstorming. This rule is especially relevant if they identify self-harm or suicide as an option. Given the ground rule, you are compelled to validate self-harm as an option and not dismiss or challenge it. However, be assured that validating suicide as an option is not the same as condoning it.

- In addition, recall that another sacrosanct ground rule is that there is always at least one pro and one con for each option. Therefore, it's important to acknowledge self-harm as an option, while also helping clients consider other options at the same time. Then you will ask clients to consider the pros and cons of every option.

- Remember, the final problem-solving ground rule is that clients always get to choose their preferred option. This raises the possibility that they might select suicide as their preferred and final option. Be assured that I have never had a young client select this as their final preferred option, so I am confident in saying that this is an unlikely outcome. However, if suicide is what the client selects and they really mean it, then you may have a very suicidal child or adolescent and should conduct a suicide risk assessment and intervention.

Problem Solving in a Crisis

• •

Use this worksheet to problem solve through a recent crisis that has triggered self-harm or suicidal urges.

Identify a self-harm or suicide trigger: _____

_____

What are some **options** to deal with this trigger? (Tip: There's no such thing as a bad option when brainstorming, even self-harm behavior.)

Option A: _____

Option B: _____

Option C: _____

What are the **pros** of each option? (Tip: There is always at least one pro for each option.)

Option A: _____

Option B: _____

Option C: _____

What are the **cons** of each option? (Tip: There is always at least one con for each option.)

Option A: _____

Option B: _____

Option C: _____

Think about your options, as well as their pros and cons, and pick the best option.

Best Option: _____

Implement the best option and see how it works. Repeat the process if it doesn't work out as planned.

CBT Skills for Self-Harm Prevention

- The following activity can be used for young clients who are (or have been) suicidal, or with young clients who engage in non-suicidal self-harm behavior (e.g., self-harm without the stated intention to die).

- Remind your clients of the basic premise of CBT and how thoughts, feelings, and behaviors are all interconnected.

- Help them map out a recent self-harm or suicide trigger and their negative thoughts, upset feelings, and unhelpful behaviors in the situation.

- Then, have them be a thought detective to find evidence for and against the stinking thinking. Help them identify some healthy, rational thinking about the situation instead.

- Review the various coping skills you've discussed with them and help them identify some healthy coping behaviors they can use to manage self-harm urges (e.g., distress tolerance skills, their safety plan, assertiveness skills, etc.).

- Help clients identify how they would likely feel if they could use positive thinking and healthy behavioral coping skills to persevere through the crisis without hurting themselves.

- Use the "Self-Harm Prevention Coping Card" to write out your client's self-harm prevention strategy. Encourage clients to keep their coping card handy and readily available. Encourage them to review it periodically and revise as needed.

CBT Skills for Self-Harm Prevention

· ·

Remember, the basic idea of CBT is that when you are in a stressful situation, you are probably having negative feelings, negative thoughts ("stinking thinking"), and negative behaviors. For example, if a girlfriend or boyfriend breaks up with you, then you might feel really depressed, you might think that your romantic relationships never work out, and you might do some self-harm behavior.

However, it doesn't have to turn out that way! CBT tells us that if you can change your stinking thinking into positive thinking – and also do some positive behaviors (instead of negative behaviors) – then you will probably solve the problem and feel a whole lot better.

For example, if a romantic partner breaks up with you, you could tell yourself that perhaps it wasn't meant to be and that you're better off without him or her (positive thinking). Then, you could call up a friend and do something fun to take your mind off of it (positive behaviors). Chances are, changing your thinking about the situation and doing some helpful behaviors is going to make you feel a lot better than if you sit and stew with your stinking thinking.

Use the following worksheets to practice using cognitive restructuring with a self-harm trigger situation that you've experienced. Then, use all of the skills and strategies that you've learned so far to develop a self-harm prevention coping card.

My Self-Harm Trigger: Stinking Thinking

· ·

Identify a stressful situation that happened to you that triggered self-harm urges. Identify the stinking thinking, upset feelings, and unhelpful behaviors that you had in this situation.

Self-Harm Trigger: _____

Stinking Thinking:

_____

_____

_____

_____

Upset Feelings:

_____

_____

_____

_____

Unhelpful Behaviors:

_____

_____

_____

_____

My Self-Harm Trigger: Be a Thought Detective

Now, be a good thought detective. Find the evidence for and against the stinking thinking for this triggering situation. Based on the evidence, identify some realistic, positive thinking about the situation, as well as some healthy coping behaviors you could do to manage the self-harm urge.

Self-Harm Trigger	Stinking Thinking	Evidence For the Stinking Thinking	Evidence Against the Stinking Thinking	Realistic, Positive Thinking	Healthy Coping Behaviors

Worksheet

My Self-Harm Prevention Coping Card

. . . .

Just like a sports team has a "game plan" that describes how they are going to win the game, it's helpful to have a plan in place that describes how to manage self-harm urges. When you have a plan in place ahead of time, it makes it easier for you to handle tough situations as they arise. Using the following coping card, develop a game plan to cope with your self-harm triggers.

Coping Card
Self-Harm Trigger: _____ _____
Consequences of Self-Harm Behavior: _____ _____
Positive Thinking: _____ _____
Positive Behavioral Coping Strategies: _____ _____
Positive Outcomes of Not Hurting Myself: _____ _____
What I Will Accept and Commit To: _____ _____

CHAPTER THIRTEEN

Parent Involvement:
Parents Are Your Clients Too!

When working with children and adolescents, it is imperative that the parents be involved in the treatment process. Developing and maintaining a positive therapeutic alliance with the parents is just as important as it is with the child or adolescent. After all, it is the parents who most likely initiated their child's treatment, and it is the parents who will pay the bills, transport the child or adolescent to and from appointments, and find time in the family's busy schedule to attend treatment sessions. In addition, it is the parents who will ultimately decide to continue or discontinue treatment for their child. You need parents to have confidence in you just as much as the child or adolescent needs to have confidence in you. Therefore, parents should not be relegated to the waiting room. They need to be involved throughout the entire process, from evaluation to termination.

As the therapist, you must gain the parents' confidence and support, as well as that of the youth, in order for treatment to be successful. You want parents to understand their child's treatment so that they can support their child in learning and using the CBT skills outside of session. In addition, there are times when the parents and child or adolescent may benefit from joint sessions so that parents can understand and learn a certain CBT skill and then reinforce use of this skill at home. There will also be times when you will need to mitigate a child-parent conflict and help parents learn effective communication, problem-solving, and positive parenting skills.

The level of parental involvement will vary with respect to the youth's age and maturity level. In general, younger clients will likely need more parental involvement. With some young children, I conduct CBT with the parent involved in nearly every session. This is especially important for kids who have anxiety and feel more comfortable with their parent in the room, or when it is critical for the parent to understand and develop some competency with a CBT skill in order to help the child use the skill effectively outside of the therapy session.

In contrast, adolescent clients will desire more privacy, which is developmentally appropriate as they seek out greater autonomy and differentiation. However, this does not mean that parents should have little or no involvement in their child's treatment. Rather, parents should generally be involved at the beginning and end of every session. This provides parents with the opportunity to report on any progress or problems before you meet with the adolescent client. Similarly, bringing parents in at the end of the session allows you to provide them with a general overview of the CBT skill addressed in session and the adolescent's homework assignment. In addition, there are times when joint family or parent-adolescent therapy will need to be done to help reduce parent-adolescent conflict and promote healthy adolescent-parent communication, problem solving, and behavioral contracting.

However, involving parents in the treatment process must always be done in accordance with confidentiality laws and ethics. A discussion of confidentiality rules is best done in the initial evaluation session so that the parent and minor client know the guiding rules right from the get-go. Having this discussion from the start will help children and adolescents open up to you with confidence, as they will feel comfortable in knowing that what they share with you will not be disclosed to their parents without their knowledge and permission.

Similarly, it will allow parents to give their children the personal space they need to fully open up to you. When having this discussion, make sure that both parents and young clients are aware of (and in agreement with) the limits of confidentiality in the event of a suicide crisis. Once clients are made aware of these confidentiality parameters, they will be better able to make their own judgment as to what they want to share or not share with you in session.

In this chapter, you'll find a number of structured activities that can help you be successful in engaging parents in their child's treatment.

Parent Involvement in the Evaluation Process

- There are several reasons that parents need to be involved in the evaluation and treatment planning process.

- Parents can provide invaluable information to complement the child's or adolescent's input and assist in assessment, diagnosis, case conceptualization, and treatment planning. In addition, parents are more likely to have confidence in a therapist who is committed to conducting an evaluation with parental input.

- Use the following outline to guide you in conducting a bio-psycho-social evaluation and diagnostic screening with the parents.

Bio-Psycho-Social Evaluation
· ·

Confidential Information

Client Name: _____   **DOB:** _____

Presenting Problem: _____

_____

Relevant History

1. Family Hx: _____

   _____

2. Psychiatric Hx: _____

   _____

3. Family Psychiatric Hx: _____

   _____

4. Developmental Hx: _____

   _____

5. Medical Hx: _____

   _____

6. Educational Hx: _____

   _____

7. Social Hx: _____

   _____

8. Trauma/Abuse Hx: _____

_____

9. Alcohol/Drug Use: _____

_____

10. Legal Hx: _____

_____

11. Sexual Development: _____

_____

Diagnostic Screen

1. Depression/Suicide: _____

_____

2. Anxiety Disorders: _____

_____

3. Obsessive Compulsive Disorder: _____

_____

4. Oppositional Defiant Disorder: _____

_____

5. Attention-Deficit/Hyperactivity Disorder: _____

_____

6. Conduct Disorder: _____

_____

7. Disruptive Mood Dysregulation Disorder: _____

_____

8. Bipolar Disorder: _____

_____

9. Specific Learning Disability: _____

_____

10. Psychosis: _____

_____

11. Eating Disorder: _____

_____

12. Autism Spectrum Disorder: _____

_____

13. Reactive Attachment Disorder: _____

_____

Strengths: _____

_____

_____

Problems: _____

_____

_____

Diagnostic Impression: _____

_____

_____

Treatment Recommendations/Plan: _____

_____

_____

_____

_____

_____

Involving the Parents in Treatment Planning

- Transparency with the parents is important throughout the course of treatment and is exemplified in the treatment planning process.

- Parents should be advised of your clinical impressions, diagnosis, case conceptualization, and treatment recommendations through a treatment planning process that involves the parents and the youth. It is important to present this information in a manner that is respectful of the parents' intimate knowledge of their child and their right to determine their child's treatment.

- Always be humble and understand that your knowledge of the child or adolescent, no matter how well-trained or experienced you may be, is still evolving and subject to error. Therefore, present your impressions and recommendations with humility by asking the parents and the youth questions such as, "Did I get this right? If not, help me get it right."

- Always identify the young client's and their family's strengths prior to identifying the child's or adolescent's problems or diagnoses.

- Be careful not to suggest that the parent is to blame for the child's/adolescent's struggles. I learned long ago, after becoming a parent myself, that parents have a very difficult job and that they are usually trying their best. They may make mistakes, but their heart is usually in the right place. Remember, the family is a complex system, and there is no single reason why the child or adolescent is struggling. My family therapy training taught me that there should never be a family scapegoat, neither the parent nor the child/adolescent. In addition, we are learning about the important role that genetics and biology play in all sorts of mental health conditions. For these reasons, always be respectful of the parent and be careful not to cast blame on them while also presenting yourself as a resource that they can use to help them be a better parent.

- Use the following outline to present your clinical impressions and treatment recommendations with the parents and the child or adolescent. Then, work with the family to develop a treatment plan that everyone agrees to.

Treatment Planning Steps

· ·

1. Describe the child's/adolescent's and their family's strengths.

2. Identify the primary problems the child/adolescent is experiencing.

3. Share your diagnostic impressions.

4. Identify the child's/adolescent's primary distress triggers.

5. Describe how the child or adolescent typically feels, thinks, and behaves when distressed.

6. Ask the parents and child/adolescent if they agree with your evaluation, diagnostic impressions, and case conceptualization. Invite them to correct or add to your impressions if needed so you "can get it right."

7. Discuss evidence-based CBT treatments for anxiety and depression. Present specific treatment recommendations for the child or adolescent framed within this CBT approach.

8. Ask them if they agree with your treatment recommendations and if they want to make a commitment to treatment.

Therapist Tips

Parent Psychoeducation

- Involving parents in the psychoeducation process is critical. Parents, as well as the child/adolescent, will benefit from having evidence-based information regarding the symptoms, prevalence, causes, and treatment of anxiety and depression.

- "Knowledge is power." Knowledge of depression and anxiety will empower parents to support their child's treatment, which ultimately benefits the child/adolescent.

- Use the psychoeducational materials presented in Chapter 2 to help parents understand depression and anxiety, as well as the respective treatments for these disorders.

- With young children, it's generally preferable to review the psychoeducational materials in a joint session with a parent present, as it helps them feel more secure and less overwhelmed.

- Adolescents often benefit from reviewing these materials in a private session, as they may feel more comfortable discussing and asking questions when their parents aren't around. However, remember to encourage adolescents to ultimately share this psychoeducational information with their parents, either in a joint session (after initially discussing it in private with you), or at home in between sessions.

Confidentiality

- The evaluation and treatment process must always be conducted in a manner consistent with applicable laws and professional ethical guidelines regarding client confidentiality.

- It is best to engage in a discussion regarding confidentiality guidelines and the limits of confidentiality during your first meeting with the child/adolescent and parent.

- With parental consent, assure the minor client that information he or she shares with you will be kept confidential unless there is imminent risk of the child or adolescent inflicting severe injury on themselves or another person, or in the case of child/adolescent endangerment.

- While ensuring confidentiality is critical to maintaining a strong therapeutic alliance with young clients, a wise clinician will understand that good communication between the youth and the parent is also a valuable clinical goal and that a young client's decision to share treatment information with the parent can be quite constructive.

- We want to preserve appropriate confidentiality while also encouraging healthy parent-child communication and collaboration in treatment.

- Use the following "Confidentiality Understanding" form to establish ground rules for sharing information provided by the minor client and involving the parent in treatment.

Confidentiality Understanding

· ·

This Confidentiality Understanding describes the terms and limits of privileged communication between the minor client and the therapist.

The minor client's discussions with the therapist will be held confidential and not released to the parent or any other party without the knowledge and consent of the minor client. However, the minor client understands that information shared with the therapist that leads the therapist to conclude that the child or adolescent is at imminent risk of engaging in serious and potentially lethal self-harm behavior, high-risk behavior that could jeopardize the child's/adolescent's life, or aggressive behavior that could potentially seriously injure someone will not be kept confidential and will be shared with the parent and possibly others in an effort to prevent the child/adolescent from engaging in the dangerous behavior.

Given the confidential nature of the minor client's communications with the therapist, the parent agrees to respect the minor child's disclosures with his or her therapist and to not pressure the child/adolescent or therapist to disclose information discussed in the minor client's treatment sessions.

The minor client also understands that good communication is part of a healthy parent-child relationship and that good parent-child communication could foster healthy collaboration in the treatment process and facilitate a positive treatment outcome. With this in mind, the minor client understands that disclosure of certain therapy issues discussed in private with the therapist could be desirable and beneficial. The minor client agrees to communicate with his or her parent about the treatment process with the understanding that the minor client can determine what treatment information to share. In addition, the minor client understands that the therapist will advise the parent of the general course of therapy (while not disclosing personal information shared in session) including the skills taught, homework assignments, and the therapist's impression of how the child/adolescent is responding to treatment, even in the absence of the minor client's consent. The parent is also entitled to inform the therapist as to the minor client's progress at home, at school, and in the community.

Child Signature: _____ Date _____

Parent Signature: _____ Date _____

Parent Involvement in Treatment Sessions

- Parents should be actively involved in the therapy sessions.

- It is good practice to meet individually with the parent(s) at the beginning of each session so they can provide an update on their child's condition and to afford them an opportunity to ask any questions that may be on their mind. At the end of the parent check-in, ask the parent if it is okay to share the parent's concerns or perspective with the child or adolescent.

- Following your session with the minor client, meet with the parent and the youth together to review important aspects of the session. With the child's or adolescent's knowledge and permission, either you or the minor client may share personal information regarding the session with the parent.

- Prior to bringing the parent in at the end of the session, always ask the client if there is anything they wish to disclose about the session.

- You can also advise the parent in general terms of the skills that were taught in the session, the minor client's responsiveness to treatment, and the child's or adolescent's homework assignment.

- A typical CBT session is outlined on the following handout as a guideline.

Typical CBT Session

. . . .

Update with parent   5 minutes

    Review progress or new information since last session

    Discuss CBT skills to be taught in current session

    Review child's/adolescent's previous homework participation

Individual session with minor client   40 minutes

    Update from child/adolescent

    Homework review

    Introduction of new CBT skill

    Practice new CBT skill

    Homework planning

Wrap-up with parent and minor client   5 minutes

    Review CBT skill taught in session

    Discuss homework

Improving Family Communication

- Children and adolescents with anxiety, depression, and suicidal tendencies, while less likely to have interactional conflict than a youth with oppositional-defiant or bipolar disorder, will nevertheless often have conflict that will require active intervention by the therapist. In order to improve family communication and resolve conflict amicably, it's helpful to have joint meetings with the minor client and parent where you can review some common family communication "mistakes" and help them develop more healthy communication skills.

- The parent(s) and child/adolescent (as well as a sibling if involved) are each given their own form to complete. Each person should self-identify the communication mistakes he or she makes and also identify the communication mistakes made by the other family members.

- Ask the minor client and parents to <u>self-identify</u> three communication mistakes they make and are willing to work on.

- Review the positive communication alternatives to develop healthy communication in the family.

- Invite each participant to identify the positive communication alternatives that they will take responsibility to work on to improve family communication. Do an experiment between sessions where each party works on correcting their communication mistakes to see if using the positive communication alternatives improves family communication.

Family Communication Skills

Identify any communication mistakes that you make, as well as any communication mistakes that other members of your family make. Each member of the family will have a chance to complete their own version of this form.

Communication Mistakes	Parent 1	Parent 2	Child	Other
1. Criticize, blame, put down				
2. Yell, raise voice, scream, swear				
3. Interrupt, shut down				
4. Lecture, preach, moralize				
5. Use a sarcastic tone of voice				
6. Mind read				
7. Get off topic				
8. Dwell, bring up the past				
9. Monopolize the conversation				
10. Threaten				
11. Become quiet, not respond, avoid				
12. Give dirty looks				
13. Deny role in the problem				

Positive Family Communication Alternatives

· ·

Circle up to three positive communication alternatives that you are willing to work on to improve family communication.

Communication Mistakes	Positive Alternatives
1. Criticize, blame, put down	Make "I" statements, balance positives and negatives, "bite your tongue"
2. Yell, raise voice, scream, swear	Speak respectfully, use a calm voice, take a "time out" to cool down, validate, empathize
3. Interrupt, shut down	Listen quietly and attentively, use "active listening"
4. Lecture, preach, moralize	Make brief, explicit statements; teach values but don't go on and on
5. Use a sarcastic tone of voice	Use a neutral or positive tone of voice
6. Mind read	Ask the other person what he or she thinks and feels
7. Get off topic	Catch yourself and return to the problem
8. Dwell, bring up the past	Catch yourself and stick to the present
9. Monopolize the conversation	Take turns talking, make brief statements, listen to the other person
10. Threaten	Stop and apologize, commit to a non-threatening discussion, take a time out, discuss when calm
11. Become quiet, not respond, avoid	Express your thoughts and feelings, be more involved, be assertive
12. Give dirty looks	Monitor your body language, maintain a positive or neutral facial expression
13. Deny role in the problem	Accept some responsibility for the problem

Therapist Tips

Family Behavioral Activation

- Behavioral activation, as described in Chapter 6, can be applied to the family as well.

- It's important to do healthy, fun activities together as a family. Quality time among family members is beneficial for all. For example, research shows that eating family meals together improves a child's or adolescent's mental and physical health.

- Invite the parents and client to develop a baseline of family-oriented activities. In a joint session, identify any activities that parents did with their child, or that the family did together, in the past month.

- Help the family discuss their values in four life areas and identify some activities that they'd like to do in each life area. Then, have them rank order these activities in terms of enjoyment.

- Identify any barriers to doing these activities (e.g., finances, time, transportation, etc.) and help the family problem solve them.

- Then, ask the parents and the youth to select and schedule one to three healthy activities that they can do with their child. Ask the parents and the child/adolescent to record how enjoyable each activity was and how they can continue doing these activities in the future.

Family Behavioral Activation

· ·

It's important to do fun and healthy activities together as a family. Doing activities together brings you closer as a family, helps you communicate better, and makes your child feel loved. As a family, identify any parent-client or family activities that you did in the past month.

Monday	Tuesday	Wednesday	Thursday	Friday	Saturday	Sunday

Family Values

. . . .

Discuss your values and interests for each of following areas, and then identify up to three activities that you can do with your child in each one of these areas.

	Activity 1	**Activity 2**	**Activity 3**
Family Relationships			
Recreation/Social			
Physical Health/Wellness			
Religion/Spirituality			

Rank order the family activities that you identified in terms of interest, with those that you enjoy most at the top of the list. Then, identify any barriers to doing them (e.g., time, money, transportation, etc.). We will work together to problem solve any barriers.

Activity (ranked by interest)	Barriers
1.	
2.	
3.	
4.	
5.	
6.	
7.	
8.	
9.	
10.	
11.	
12.	

Activity Selection and Monitoring

· ·

Using your answers from the "Family Values" worksheet, select three activities that you agree to do in the near future. Plan out when and how you will do these activities. After you do these activities, rate how much you enjoyed each activity on a 1 to 10 scale (higher rating = more enjoyment). Then, identify anything you can do that might improve the activity in the future. Finally, discuss how you might continue doing the activity.

	Activity 1 _____	**Activity 2** _____	**Activity 3** _____
Date and time we will do the activity:			
How much we enjoyed the activity (1-10):			
Is there anything we can do to improve the activity in the future? If so, what?			
How can we continue doing this activity?			

Family Problem Solving

- All families will inevitably have some conflict. Family conflict is quite normal, really. However, it's critical to resolve conflicts as they emerge, as unresolved conflict is detrimental to all family members.

- In order to improve the family's problem-solving skills, hold a joint session where you ask the parents and the child/adolescent to discuss and identify a specific problem within the family unit. Remind them to describe the problem using objective, non-judgmental language.

- Brainstorm at least three options that would provide a solution to this problem. (Remember, there's no such thing as a bad option when brainstorming.)

- Discuss the pros and cons of each option. (Remember, there is always at least one pro and one con for every option.)

- Have each family member rank order the options according to their preference.

- See if there is an option that everyone agrees on (a "win-win" solution), or one that the majority agrees on. If they can't find a solution that they all agree on, then the parents make the final decision, as they are the natural leaders of the family.

Family Problem Solving

· ·

Use this worksheet to problem solve and work through a recent family conflict you have been experiencing.

Identify the problem you are having as a family (be specific and non-judgmental): _____

_____

What are three possible **options** to deal with this problem? (Tip: There's no such thing as a bad option when brainstorming.)

    Option A: _____

    Option B: _____

    Option C: _____

What are the **pros** of each option? (Tip: There is always at least one pro for each option.)

    Option A: _____

    Option B: _____

    Option C: _____

What are the **cons** of each option? (Tip: There is always at least one con for each option.)

    Option A: _____

    Option B: _____

    Option C: _____

Rank order these options in terms of preference (1 = most preferred; 2 = second best; 3 = least preferred).

Possible Options	Parent 1	Parent 2	Child
Option A:			
Option B:			
Option C:			

Now, pick the best option. Is there one you all agree on? (Parents always have the tie breaker.)

Best Option: _____

How will you implement this option? _____

_____

_____

Implement the solution and see if it helps.

Family Behavioral Contract

- Children and adolescents who struggle with depression and anxiety will, at times, exhibit disruptive or unhealthy behaviors. When this occurs, a family behavioral contract can be quite helpful in resolving these problematic behaviors.

- Develop a family behavioral contract to resolve a specific problem behavior that the child or adolescent is having.

- Identify the child's/adolescent's contribution to the problem and what he or she will do differently to resolve the problem.

- To avoid scapegoating the child or adolescent, identify the parents' contribution to the problem and their responsibility in resolving it. Doing so is very important and empowering for the child/ adolescent. I remember a case when a child wanted to give the parent a "sad face" for yelling. The parent looked intimidated, so I looked at the parent and said, "That's only 'even-steven,' isn't it?" and everyone laughed and agreed.

- Identify the rewards and consequences for the child or adolescent for meeting, or failing to meet, the terms of the contract.

- Identify how the youth can address the parents if they are not following through with their responsibilities. I usually encourage the child/adolescent to report on how parents are doing with their responsibility in a joint session at subsequent meetings (that's only "even-steven").

Family Behavioral Contract

· ·

Identify a specific problem that the child or adolescent is experiencing: _____

_____

The child's/adolescent's contribution to the problem: _____

_____

The child's/adolescent's responsibility (what he or she will do to help resolve the problem):

_____

The parent's contribution to the problem: _____

_____

The parent's responsibility (what parents will do to help resolve the problem): _____

_____

If the child/adolescent is compliant with this contract, he or she will earn the following: _____

_____

If the child/adolescent is not compliant with this contract, the consequence will be: _____

_____

If parents are not following through with their responsibility, the child/adolescent may address the
situation by: _____

_____

All parties have discussed and understand this agreement.

Child Signature: _____

Parent Signature: _____

Date: _____

Parent Support and Stress Management

- Parents experience a great deal of stress when their child is experiencing depression or anxiety, and especially if their child is exhibiting self-harm or suicidal urges. Therefore, it's important that parents receive support in the context of treatment as well (Family Connections Program, 2019).

- One way to support parents is to ensure that they are using stress management skills to re-charge their batteries and be helpful to their child when needed. The following worksheet asks parents to identify several activities that they can do in order to ensure that they are receiving enough support and keeping their stress levels in check.

- One important stress management tool for parents involves setting needed limits with their child. However, some parents may be reluctant to do so, as they fear that setting limits with a child who self-harms may trigger a crisis and self-harm behavior. It's important to reassure the parents that failure to set needed limits will only increase their child's likelihood of problems. It is important to support the parent's legitimate authority and responsibility in setting needed limits with their child. The family problem-solving and behavioral contract interventions presented earlier in this chapter can be helpful in this regard.

- Parents can also benefit from individual stress management counseling to help them manage the stress involved in raising a child or adolescent who is prone to depression, anxiety, and/or self-harm.

Parent Support and Stress Management Skills

· ·

Parents need to take proper care of themselves in order to provide their children with the critical support they need. Identify how you can take care of yourself so you have the energy to help your child when needed.

☐ Utilize my child's safety plan if needed

☐ Enforce limits as needed

☐ Use family problem solving

☐ Develop a family behavioral contract

☐ Take a time out to stay calm and composed as needed

☐ Practice mindfulness with deep breathing, meditation, visualization, etc.

☐ Spend quality time with my spouse

☐ Spend quality time with my child despite his or her struggles

☐ Socialize with friends

☐ Engage in regular physical exercise

☐ Enjoy a hobby (e.g., book club, athletic activity, music, painting, etc.)

☐ Join a community organization

☐ Ensure time to relax

☐ Attend to the needs of my other children

☐ Spend quality time with my other children

☐ Join a support group

☐ Get proper sleep

☐ Practice good nutrition

☐ Take time to notice and validate my thoughts, feelings, and behaviors on a regular basis

☐ Other: _____

References

Albano, A. M., & DiBartolo, P. M. (2007). *Cognitive-behavioral therapy for social phobia in adolescents: Stand up, speak out* (1st ed.). New York, NY: Oxford University Press.

Beck, A., Rush, A., Shaw, B., & Emery, G. (1979). *Cognitive therapy of depression.* New York, NY: Guilford Press.

Brent, D. A., Poling, K. D., & Goldstein, T. R. (2011). *Treating depressed and suicidal adolescents.* New York, NY: Guilford Press.

Centers for Disease Control and Prevention. (2018). *Suicide: Risk and protective factors.* Retrieved from https://www.cdc.gov/violenceprevention/suicide/riskprotectivefactors.html

Clarke, G., Lewinsohn, P., & Hops, H. (1990). *Leader's manual for adolescent groups: Adolescent coping with depression course.* Portland, OR: Kaiser Permanente Center for Health Research.

Cohen, J.A., Mannarino, A.P. and Deblinger, E. (Eds.) (2016). *Trauma-Focused CBT for children and adolescents: Treatment applications.* New York, NY: Guilford Press.

Curry, J. F., Wells, K. C., Brent, D. A., Clarke, G. N., Rohde, P., Albana, A. M., ... Kolker, J. (2000). *Treatment for Adolescents with Depression Study (TADS): Cognitive behavior therapy manual. Introduction, rationale, and adolescent sessions.* Durham, NC: Duke University Medical Center.

Curtin, S. C., Heron, M., Miniño, A. M., & Warner, M. (2018). Recent increases in injury mortality among children and adolescents aged 10–19 years in the United States: 1999–2016. *Centers for Disease Control and Prevention, National Vital Statistics Report, 67(4)*, 1–16.

Family Connections Program. (2019). Retrieved from www.borderlinepersonalitydisorder.com/family-connections/

Fennell, M.J. & Teasdale, J.D. (1987). Cognitive Therapy for Depression: Individual differences and the process of change. *Cognitive Therapy and Research. 11*, 253-271

Friedberg, R. D., & McClure, J. M. (2015). *Clinical practice of cognitive therapy with children and adolescents: The nuts and bolts.* New York, NY: Guilford Press.

Gudmundsen, G., McCauley, E., Schloredt, K., Martell, C., Rhew, I., Hubley, S., & Dimidjian, S. (2016). The Adolescent Behavioral Activation Program: Adapting behavioral activation as a treatment for depression in adolescence. *Journal of Clinical Child & Adolescent Psychology, 45(3)*, 291–304.

Hayes, S. C., Strosahl, K. D., & Wilson, K. G. (2011). *Acceptance and commitment therapy: The process and practice of mindful change* (2nd ed.). New York, NY: Guilford Press.

Heron, M. (2018). Deaths: Leading causes for 2016. *Centers for Disease Control and Prevention, National Vital Statistics Report, 67(6)*, 1–76.

Ireland, T. (2014, June 12). What does mindfulness meditation do to your brain? *Scientific American.* Retrieved from https://blogs.scientificamerican.com/guest-blog/what-does-mindfulness-meditation-do-to-your-brain/

Kendall, P. C., Crawford, E. A., Kagan, E. R., Furr, J. M., & Podell, J. L. (2017). Child-focused treatment for anxiety. In J. R. Weiz & A. E. Kazdin (Eds.), *Evidenced-based psychotherapies for children and adolescents* (3rd ed., pp. 17–34). New York, NY: Guilford Press.

Levy, R. L., Langer, S. L., Walker, L. S., Romano, J. M., Christie, D. L., Youseff, N., ... Whitehead, W. E. (2011). Cognitive behavioral therapy for children with functional abdominal pain and their parents decreases pain and other symptoms. *American Journal of Gastroenterology, 105(4)*, 946–956.

Linehan, M. (1993). *Cognitive-behavioral treatment of borderline personality disorder.* New York, NY: Guilford Press.

Mahler, M., Pine, S., & Bergman, A. (2008). *The psychological birth of the human infant: Symbiosis and individuation.* New York, NY: Basic Books.

March, J., Silva, S., Curry, J., Wells, K., Fairbank, J., Burns, B., … Bartoi, M. (2009). The Treatment for Adolescents with Depression Study (TADS): Outcomes over 1 year of naturalistic follow-up. *American Journal of Psychiatry, 166*(10), 1141–1149.

O'Hara, M. W., & Rehm, L. P. (1979). Self-monitoring, activity levels, and mood in the development and maintenance of depression. *Journal of Abnormal Psychology, 88*(4), 450–453.

Piaget, J. (1969). *The psychology of the child.* New York, NY: Basic Books.

Posner, K., Brown, G. K., Stanley, B., Brent, D. A., Yershova, K. V., Oquendo, M. A., … Mann, J. J. (2011). The Columbia-Suicide Severity Rating Scale: Initial validity and internal consistency findings from three multisite studies with adolescents and adults. *The American Journal of Psychiatry, 168*(12), 1266–77.

Pratt, D. M. (2008, October). *The Mood Management Program: An open clinical trial with severely depressed and suicidal adolescents.* Paper presented at the Kansas Conference in Clinical Child Psychology, Lawrence, KS.

Resick, P. A., Monson, C. M., & Chard, K. M. (2016). *Cognitive processing therapy for PTSD: A comprehensive manual.* New York, NY: Guilford Press.

Sanchez, V. C., Lewinsohn, P., & Larson, D. W. (1980). Assertiveness training: Effectiveness in treating depression. *Journal of Clinical Psychology, 36*(2), 526–529.

Satterfield, J. M. (2015). *Cognitive behavioral therapy: Techniques for retraining your brain.* Chantilly, VA: The Great Courses.

Seligman, M. (1996). *The optimistic child.* New York, NY: Houghton Mifflin.

Stanley, B., & Brown, G. K. (2012). Safety planning intervention: A brief intervention to mitigate suicide risk. *Cognitive and Behavioral Practice, 19,* 256–264

Teasdale, J., & Williams, M. (2014). *The mindful way workbook: An 8-week program to free yourself from depression and emotional distress.* New York, NY: Guilford Press.

Tindall, L., Mikocka-Walus, A., McMillan, D., Wright, B., Hewitt, C., & Gascoyne, S. (2017). Is behavioral activation effective in the treatment of depression in young people? A systematic review and meta-analysis. *Psychology and Psychotherapy: Theory, Research and Practice, 90*(4), 770–796.

Wampold, B., & Imel, Z. E. (2015). *The great psychotherapy debate: The evidence for what makes psychotherapy work.* New York, NY: Routledge.

Weisz, J. R., & Kazdin, A. E. (Eds.). (2017). *Evidenced-based psychotherapies for children and adolescents* (3rd ed.). New York, NY: Guilford Press.

Resources

For your convenience, purchasers can download and print worksheets and handouts from www.pesi.com/pratt

Abela, J. R. Z., & Hankin, B. L. (Eds.). (2008). *Handbook of depression in children and adolescents.* New York, NY: Guilford Press.

A-Tjak, J. G., Davis, M. L., Morina, N., Powers, M. B., Smits, J. A., & Emmelkamp, P. M. (2015). A meta-analysis of the efficacy of acceptance and commitment therapy for clinically relevant mental health and physical health problems. *Psychotherapy and Psychosomatics, 84,* 30–36.

Barkley, R., & Robin, A. (2014). *Defiant teens: A clinician's manual for assessment and family intervention.* New York, NY: Guilford Press.

Barnard, P., & Teasdale, A. (1993). *Affect, cognition and change: Re-modelling depressive thought.* New York, NY: Psychology Press.

Berman, A. L., Jobes, D. A., & Silverman, M. M. (2006). *Adolescent suicide assessment and intervention* (2nd ed.). Washington, DC: American Psychological Association.

Boy's Town Press. (2005). *Solving problems: SODAS method.* Retrieved from https://boystowntraining.org/assets/sodatechniques.pdf

Brent, D. A., Greenhill, L. L., Compton, S., Emslie, G., Wells, K., Walkup, J. T., ... Turner, J. B. (2009). The Treatment of Adolescent Suicide Attempters Study (TASA): Predictors of suicidal events in an open treatment trial. *Journal of the American Academy of Child and Adolescent Psychiatry, 48*(10), 987–996.

Center for Behavioral Health Statistics and Quality. (2016). *2015 national survey on drug use and health: Detailed tables.* Rockville, MD: Substance Abuse and Mental Health Services Administration.

Centers for Disease Control. (2017). QuickStats: Suicide rates for teens aged 15–19 years, by sex–United States, 1975–2015. *Morbidity and Mortality Weekly Report (MMWR), 66,* 816.

Clarke, G., Hyman, H., Lewinsohn, P. M., Andrews, J., Seeley, J. R., & Williams, J. (1992). Cognitive-behavioral group treatment of adolescent depression: Prediction of outcome. *Behavior Therapy, 23*(3), 341–354.

Curry, J., Silva, S., Rohde, P., Ginsburg, G., Kratochvil, C., Simons, A., ... March, J. (2011). Recovery and recurrence following treatment for adolescent major depression. *Archives of General Psychiatry, 68*(3), 263–269.

Ellis, A., & Harper, R. A. (1961). *A guide to rational living.* Englewood Cliffs, NJ: Institute for Rational Living.

Fonagy, P., Cottrell, D., Phillips, J., Bevington, D., Glaser, D., & Allison, E. (2015). *What works for whom: A critical review of treatments for children and adolescents.* New York, NY: Guilford Press.

Forgatch, M. S., & Gewirtz, A. H. (2018). The evolution of the Oregon Model of parent management training: An intervention for antisocial behavior in children and adolescents. In J. R. Weisz & A. E. Kazdin (Eds.), *Evidence-based psychotherapies for children and adolescents* (pp. 85–102). New York, NY: Guilford Press.

Hoffman, S. G., Asnaani, A., Vonk, I. J., Sawyer, A. T., & Fang, A. (2012). The efficacy of cognitive-behavioral therapy: A review of meta-analyses. *Cognitive Therapy and Research, 36*(5), 427–440.

Horowitz, L. M., Bridge, J. A., Teach, S. J., Ballard, E., Klima, J., Rosenstein, D. L., ... Pao, M. (2012). Ask Suicide-Screening Questions (ASQ): A brief instrument for the pediatric emergency department. *Archives of Pediatrics & Adolescent Medicine, 166*(12), 1170–1176.

Kabat-Zinn, J. (1994). *Wherever you go, there you are. Mindfulness meditation in everyday life.* New York, NY: Hyperion Books.

Kaplan, K. A., & Harvey, A. G. (2014). Treatment of sleep disturbance. In D. H. Barlow (Ed.), *Clinical handbook of psychological disorders: A step-by-step treatment manual* (pp. 640–669). New York, NY: Guilford Press.

Kennard, B. D., Hughes, J. L., & Foxwell, A. F. (2016). *CBT for depression in children and adolescents: A guide to relapse prevention*. New York, NY: Guilford Press.

Lejuez, C. W., Hopko, D. R., Acierno, R., Daughters, S. B., & Pagoto, S. L. (2011). Ten year revision of the Brief Behavioral Activation Treatment for Depression: Revised treatment manual. *Behavior Modification, 35*(2), 111–161.

Lewinsohn, P. M. (1975). The behavioral study and treatment of depression. *Progress in Behavioral Modification, 1,* 19–65.

March, J., Silva, S., Petrycki, S., Curry, J., Wells, K., Fairbank, J., ... Kennard, B. (2007). The Treatment for Adolescents with Depression Study (TADS): Long-term effectiveness and safety outcomes. *Archives of General Psychiatry, 64*(10), 1132–1144.

Milkowitz, D. J., & George, E. L. (2008). *The bipolar teen: What you can do to help your child and your family*. New York, NY: Guilford Press.

Öst, L. G. (2014). The efficacy of acceptance and commitment therapy: An updated systematic review and meta-analysis. *Behaviour Research and Therapy, 61,* 105–121.

Persons, J. B. (2008). *The case formulation approach to cognitive behavior therapy*. New York, NY: Guilford Press.

Piet, J., & Hougaard, E. (2011). The effect of mindfulness-based cognitive therapy for prevention of relapse in recurrent major depressive disorder: A systematic review and meta-analysis. *Clinical Psychology Review, 31*(6), 1032–1040.

Rathus, J. H., & Miller, A. L. (2014). *DBT skills manual for adolescents*. New York, NY: Guilford Press.

Resick, P. A., Monson, C. M., & Chard, K. M. (2016). *Cognitive processing therapy for PTSD: A comprehensive manual*. New York, NY: Guilford Press.

Sears, R. (2017). *Cognitive behavioral therapy & mindfulness toolbox: 50 tips, tools, and handouts for anxiety, stress, depression, personality and mood disorder*. Eau Claire, WI: PESI Publishing & Media.

Segal, Z. V. (2016, June 8). *Guided practice: Three-minute breathing space* [Video file]. Retrieved from https://youtu.be/amX1IuYFv8A

Spates, C. R., Pagoto, S. L., & Kalata, A. (2006). A qualitative and quantitative review of behavioral activation treatment of major depressive disorder. *The Behavior Analyst Today, 7*(4), 508–521.

Stanley, B., Brown, G. K., Currier, G. W., Lyons, C., Chesin, M., & Knox, K. L. (2015). Brief intervention and follow-up for suicidal patients with repeat emergency department visits enhances treatment engagement. *American Journal of Public Health, 105*(8), 1570–1572.

Sullivan, E. M., Annest, J. L., Simon, T. R., Luo, F., & Dahlberg, L. L. (2015). Suicide trends among persons aged 10–24 years — United States, 1994–2012. *Morbidity and Mortality Weekly Report, 64*(8), 201–205.

Twenge, J. M., Martin, G. N., & Campbell, W. K. (2018). Decreases in psychological well-being among American adolescents after 2012 and links to screen time during the rise of smartphone technology. *Emotion, 18*(6), 765–780.

Velting, O. N., Setzer, N. J., & Albano, A. M. (2004). Update on and advances in assessment and cognitive-behavioral treatment of anxiety disorders in children and adolescents. *Professional Psychology Research and Practice, 35*(1), 42–54.

Wasserman, D., Hoven, C. W., Wasserman, C., Wall, M., Eisenberg, R., Hadlaczky, G., ... Carli, V. (2015). School-based suicide prevention programs: The SEYLE clustered randomized, controlled trial. *Lancet, 385*(9977), 1536–1544.

Zero Suicide. (2013). *Suicide planning intervention for suicide prevention*. Retrieved from http://zerosuicide.sprc.org/sites/zerosuicide.sprc.org/files/sp/course.htm

Personal and Family History	Personal	Family	Notes
Abuse — *continued*			
sexual	V15.41		Subcategory VI5.4 excludes history of conditions classifiable to 290-316 (see V11.0-V11.9)
Affective psychosis	V11.1	V17.0	V11.1 includes personal history of manic-depressive psychosis
			V17.0 excludes family history of mental retardation (see code V18.4)
Alcoholism	V11.3	V61.41	V17.0 excludes family history of mental retardation (see code V18.4)
Allergy to			
analgesic agent NEC	V14.6	V19.6	
anesthetic NEC	V14.4	V19.6	
antibiotic agent NEC	V14.1	V19.6	
anti-infective agent NEC	V14.3	V19.6	
arachnid bite	V15.06	V19.6	
diathesis	V15.09	V19.6	
drug allergy	V14.9	V19.6	
drug allergy, specified type NEC	V14.8	V19.6	
eggs	V15.03	V19.6	
food additives	V15.05	V19.6	
insect bite	V15.06	V19.6	
latex	V15.07	V19.6	
medicinal agents	V14.9	V19.6	
medicinal agents, specified type NEC	V14.8	V19.6	
milk products	V15.02	V19.6	
narcotic agent NEC	V14.5	V19.6	
nuts	V15.05	V19.6	
peanuts	V15.01	V19.6	
penicillin	V14.0	V19.6	
radiographic dye	V15.08	V19.6	
seafood	V15.04	V19.6	
serum	V14.7	V19.6	
specified food NEC	V15.05	V19.6	
specified nonmedicinal agents NEC	V15.09	V19.6	
spider bite	V15.06	V19.6	
sulfa	V14.2	V19.6	
sulfonamides	V14.2	V19.6	
therapeutic agent	V15.09	V19.6	
vaccine	V14.7	V19.6	
Anaphylactic shock	V15.09		
Anaphylaxis	V13.81	V19.6	
Anemia	V12.3	V18.2	For family history of other blood disorders, see code V18.3
Anomaly (corrected)			
circulatory system	V13.65	V19.5	
cleft lip, palate	V13.64	V19.5	V13.64 also includes malformations (corrected) of eye, ear, face and neck
digestive system	V13.67	V19.5	
genitourinary system	V13.62	V19.5	
musculoskeletal system	V13.68	V19.5	V13.68 includes malformations of integument and limbs
nervous system	V13.63	V19.5	
respiratory system	V13.66	V19.5	
Arrest, sudden cardiac	V12.53	V17.41	V12.5 excludes old myocardial infarction (412) and postmyocardial infarction syndrome (411.0)
			V12.53 includes successfully resuscitated sudden cardiac death
Arteriosclerosis (cardiovascular)	code to condition	V17.49	
Arthritis	V13.4	V17.7	
Asthma	code to condition	V17.5	
attack, transient ischemic (TIA)	V12.54	V17.1	V12.54 includes unspecified stroke without residual deficits
Benign neoplasm of brain	V12.41		
Blindness	code to condition	V19.0	
Blood disease	V12.3	V18.3	
Calculi, urinary	V13.01	V18.7	
Cardiovascular disease	V12.50	V17.49	
myocardial infarction	412	V17.3	
Carrier, genetic disease	V83.01-V83.89	V18.9	See category V84 for Genetic susceptibility to disease
Chemotherapy, antineoplastic	V87.41		V87.41 excludes long-term current drug use(see codes V58.61-V58.69)
Child abuse	V15.41		
Chronic respiratory condition NEC	V12.60	V17.6	
Cigarette smoking	V15.82		V15.82 excludes tobacco dependence (see code 305.1)
Circulatory system disease	V12.50	V17.3	V12.5 excludes old myocardial infarction (412) and postmyocardial infarction syndrome (411.0)
myocardial infarction	412	V17.3	

Personal and Family History

Personal and Family History	Personal	Family	Notes
Colonic polyps	V12.72	V18.51	
Combat and operational stress reaction	V11.4		
Congenital (corrected) **malformation**	V13.69	V19.5	
circulatory system	V13.65	V19.5	
digestive system	V13.67	V19.5	
ear	V13.64	V19.5	
eye	V13.64	V19.5	
face	V13.64	V19.5	
genitourinary system	V13.62	V19.5	
heart	V13.65	V19.5	
hypospadias	V13.61	V19.5	
integument (skin)	V13.68	V19.5	
limbs	V13.68	V19.5	
lip (cleft)	V13.64	V19.5	
musculsoskeletal	V13.68	V19.59	
nervous system	V13.63	V19.5	
palate (cleft)	V13.64	V19.5	
respiratory system	V13.66	V19.5	
specified type	V13.69	V19.5	
Consanguinity		V19.7	
Contact (exposure) (suspected)			
asbestos	V15.84		
bodily fluids, potentially hazardous	V15.85		
lead	V15.86		
Contraception	V15.7		
Coronary artery disease	V12.50	V17.3	V12.5 excludes old myocardial infarction (412) and postmyocardial infarction syndrome (411.0)
Cystic fibrosis	V12.69	V18.19	
Deafness	code to condition	V19.2	
Death, sudden, successfully resuscitated	V12.53	V17.41	V12.5 excludes old myocardial infarction (412) and postmyocardial infarction syndrome (411.0)
Deficit			
prolonged reversible ischemic neurologic (PRIND)	V12.54	V17.1, V17.2	V12.54 includes unspecified stroke without residual deficits
reversible ischemic neurologic (RIND)	V12.54	V17.1, V17.2	V12.54 includes unspecified stroke without residual deficits
Diabetes mellitus	code to condition	V18.0	
gestational	V12.21	V18.0	
Diathesis, allergic	V15.09	V19.6	
Digestive system disease	V12.70	V18.59	
peptic ulcer	V12.71	V18.59	
polyps, colonic	V12.72	V18.51	For family history of malignant neoplasm of gastrointestinal tract see code V16.0
specified NEC	V12.79	V18.59	
Disease (of)	V13.9	V19.8	
blood	V12.3	V18.3	
blood-forming organs	V12.3	V18.3	
cardiovascular system	V12.50	V17.49	
cerebrovascular system	V12.59	V17.2	
circulatory system	V12.50	V17.1, V17.3	
circulatory, specified NEC	V12.59	V17.1	
coronary artery	V12.50	V17.3	V12.5 excludes old myocardial infarction (412) and postmyocardial infarction syndrome (411.0)
digestive system	V12.70	V18.59	
peptic ulcer	V12.71	V18.59	
polyps, colonic	V12.72	V18.51	For family history of malignant neoplasm of gastrointestinal tract see code V16.0
digestive, specified NEC	V12.79	V18.59	
ear NEC	V12.49	V19.3	
eye NEC	V12.49	V19.19	
glaucoma	code to condition	V19.11	
hypertensive	V12.59	V17.49	
infectious	V12.00	V18.8	
malaria	V12.03	V18.8	
methicillin resistant Staphylococcus aureus (MRSA) V12.04	V12.04	V18.8	
MRSA (methicillin resistant Staphylococcus aureus) V12.04	V12.04	V18.8	
poliomyelitis	V12.02	V18.8	